At Issue

The Wireless Society

Other Books in the At Issue Series:

At Issue

The Wireless Society

Stuart A. Kallen, Book Editor

GREENHAVEN PRESS

An imprint of Thomson Gale, a part of The Thomson Corporation

Detroit • New York • San Francisco • New Haven, Conn. • Waterville, Maine • London

Christine Nasso, *Publisher*
Elizabeth Des Chenes, *Managing Editor*

© 2007 Thomson Gale, a part of The Thomson Corporation.

Thomson and Star logo are trademarks and Gale and Greenhaven Press are registered trademarks used herein under license.

For more information, contact:
Greenhaven Press
27500 Drake Rd.
Farmington Hills, MI 48331-3535
Or you can visit our Internet site at http://www.gale.com

LIBRARY OF CONGRESS CATALOGING-IN-PUBLICATION DATA

The wireless society / Stuart A. Kallen, book editor.
   p. cm. -- (At issue)
Includes bibliographical references and index.
ISBN-13: 978-0-7377-2749-4 (lib. : alk. paper)
ISBN-10: 0-7377-2749-7 (lib. : alk. paper)
ISBN-13: 978-0-7377-2750-0 (pbk. : alk. paper)
ISBN-10: 0-7377-2750-0 (pbk. : alk. paper)
1. Wireless LANs--Juvenile literature. 2. Cellular telephone systems--Juvenile literature. 3. Wireless communication systems--Social aspects--Juvenile literature.
I. Kallen, Stuart A., 1955-
TK5105.78.W6655 2006
004.6'8--dc22

                                    2006028629

Printed in the United States of America
10 9 8 7 6 5 4 3 2 1

Contents

Introduction

Today over 203 million people in the United States—about two-thirds of the population—own a cell phone. The popularity of wireless Internet access is also skyrocketing: Every day about one in three Americans—100 million people—log onto the Net using wireless local area networks (WLANs) and wireless devices that meet industry standards commonly known as wi-fi. With wi-fi technology little more than five years old, and commercial cellular technology barely two decades old, these statistics leave little doubt that the United States has become a wireless society in a very short time.

One could say the wireless society began in 1983, when the Federal Communications Commission (FCC) approved the first commercial cellular telephone, Motorola's DynaTAC 8000X, a foot-long model that weighed almost two pounds. Although the bulky phone was compared to a brick, consumers immediately recognized its convenience and other advantages over the old stationary, vehicle-installed mobile phones. In Chicago and Washington, D.C., where wireless networks were first installed, about 340,000 people purchased the new cellular phones at $3,500 a piece.

By the early 1990s cell phones had become considerably smaller and cheaper. In 1995 nearly 33 million Americans were enjoying wireless communications. Eight years later that number had grown to 158 million people. In a few short years, technology once viewed as a luxury had come to be considered a necessity by the majority of Americans of all walks of life. This ongoing technological revolution has had both positive and negative consequences and has raised questions about safety, security, and even simple etiquette that have yet to be answered.

Many people initially purchase cell phones for personal security. According to the Cellular Telecommunications and Internet Association, 90 percent of those polled in 2001 said they felt safer when carrying a cell phone. And there is no doubt that the phones are useful in reaching help in emergency situations: Every day, nearly 175,000 emergency calls are made from cell phones.

Many parents also consider cell phones an essential way to keep in touch with their children. In 2006 an estimated 75 percent of middle school students carried cell phones, as did close to 90 percent of high school students. Increasingly, parents are buying cell phones with built-in Global Positioning System (GPS) chips for children as young as five years old to carry. Via the Internet, a parent can locate such a GPS-equipped cell phone anywhere, with pinpoint accuracy, to track children's movements and make sure they are safely at school or at a friend's house.

Another service, called geofencing, allows parents to program a child's phone with geographic boundaries, such as an area around a school. When a child leaves the area, the parent receives a text message. Employers also use these phones to monitor the whereabouts and activities of their employees. This aspect of the wireless revolution, however, is raising concerns about privacy and other civil liberties. Pam Dickey, who works for a San Francisco company that requires workers to carry such a phone, explains: "We hardly have any privacy as it is now—you go to a gas station and there's a camera on you, there are cameras outside of residential homes. . . . Now you have a telephone that will . . . tell people where you are, too—when you're in the bathroom, and how long you're there. It's too much an invasion of privacy."

Some would argue that their own privacy is being violated when cell phone users carry on impossible-to-ignore conversations in public places. These so-called cell yellers have become a common annoyance in restaurants and on airplanes, subways, and sidewalks. As Christine Rosen writes in the *New Atlantis*: "I've heard business deals, lovers' quarrels, and the most unsavory gossip. I've listened to strangers discuss in excruciating detail their own and others' embarrassing medical conditions; I've heard the details of recent real estate purchases, job triumphs, and awful dates."

Another kind of privacy is a concern of wi-fi computer users, some of whom are unwittingly sharing intimate details of their lives over the Internet. For example, hackers with criminal intent can use inexpensive hardware and software tools to locate and penetrate WLANs and steal passwords, read e-mail messages, or launch attacks on other computers. Despite the risks, public demand is strong for televisions, CD players, video recorders, personal organizers, and other devices that are wi-fi compatible, and consumer electronics companies are competing to develop new products that attract the eager buyer's attention.

Likewise, the latest high-tech cell phones are loaded with features including a video camera, a 1.2-megapixel still camera, a speakerphone, and removable memory. Like other wireless technologies, these features are provoking controversy. For example, cell phone cameras have already been used to take surreptitious photographs of the occupants of restrooms and locker rooms—images that were later posted on the Internet without subjects' consent. Cell phone video cameras will presumably be used in the same manner, especially as ever-tinier models reach the market.

Whatever its drawbacks, however, wireless technology has provided countless benefits to society. It allows doctors to communicate with and diagnose patients in rural or inaccessible areas. Workers in the field can instantly transmit detailed photographs of an accident site or work in progress to managers in distant offices. And billions of people every day use wireless to shop, stay in touch with friends and family, and access up-to-the minute news, weather, and traffic reports. Wireless technology has transformed modern society in ways that people would have considered incredible only thirty years ago. Few such technological revolutions in history have been as rapid or as profound.

1

Municipal Wi-Fi Is Part of a Communications Revolution

Neal Peirce

Neal Peirce is a syndicated columnist based in Washington, D.C. His weekly column, which appears in more than fifty newspapers nationwide, examines trends and innovations in state and local government.

Wireless local area networks, or wi-fi, is a revolutionary technology that is allowing city governments to offer incredibly cheap broadband Internet service to its citizens. By installing wireless transmitters on utility poles, municipal wi-fi providers are linking businesses, schools, museums, and citizens on every economic level. Although the number of wi-fi "hot spots" is growing daily at coffee shops, restaurants, and hotels, urban wi-fi is creating "hot cities" that can spread economic opportunity in poor neighborhoods while allowing civic leaders to promote local culture and improve government services. There is a revolution in the air and it is coming from the invisible wi-fi transmitters that are linking Americans as never before.

Philadelphia is debating making all 134 square miles of the city the world's largest wireless hotspot. Boston, Atlanta, New York, Los Angeles and other cities are considering parallel moves. In Europe, the firm HotSpot Amsterdam is set to go citywide in the Dutch capital soon.

A OneCleveland campaign, led by Case Western Reserve University, boasts of the thousands of users already logged

Neal Peirce, "Whole Cities as Internet Hotspots? The Wifi Revolution Spreads," *Government Finance Review*, vol. 20, December 2004, pp. 62–63. Copyright © 2004 The Washington Post Writers Group. Reproduced by permission.

cost-free onto rapid broadband Internet service through the 4,000 wireless transmitters recently installed in the University Circle and Midtown districts and along the lakefront.

From Corpus Christi, Texas, to the Silicon Valley, at least 50 cities are actively exploring their own versions of remarkably inexpensive community-wide transmitter nets, mounted every few hundred feet on utility poles and light posts. The new technology, called WiFi (shorthand for wireless fidelity), is increasingly popular as manufacturers build receiver chips into laptops and handheld computers.

The broadcast costs are amazingly low. The estimate for mounting a network serving all of Philadelphia and its 1.5 million people, for example, is just $10 million, or less than $7 a person. "This comes as close to a free lunch as I've ever seen in my years watching technology," says Costis Toregas, recently retired president of Public Technology Inc. in Washington, D.C.

City governments are logical WiFi network initiators and anchor users, creating instant low-cost communications systems for every function from police reporting to meter reading, video surveillance to disaster management.

Yet once a city network is built, the same equipment can easily provide Internet service, including all manner of e-government services and free or low-cost Web service. Users include lower-income students and struggling small businesses likely to find normal commercial broadband service ($35 to $65 monthly) unaffordable.

Just this month [December 2004], little Chaska, Minn., is shaking up the high-speed Internet providers by offering all its 7,000 homes city-run wireless broadband Internet for $16 monthly.

Hot Spots to Hot Cities

But there's no set formula on how community-wide WiFi will develop, says Toregas. Government may be an initiator, but it's not always good at the challenges of deployment, marketing and maintenance required. So look for a period of intense experimentation with multiple partners—private providers, utilities, chambers of commerce, neighboring communities, schools and universities all playing roles.

They want to create a national model of applying WiFi technology to bolster culture, advance learning, better health services, and spread economic opportunity to pockets of extreme poverty.

The progression from "hot spots" such as Internet cafes to "hot cities" will quickly have to jump traditional borders to "hot regions," notes community communications expert Seth Fearey of Joint Venture Silicon Valley. As opposed to radio and TV stations and cell phone operations, WiFi operates on unlicensed frequency spectrum. This allows for fast experimentation, but also potentially jammed or overlapping signals if one city picks one vendor and its neighbor another.

So "it's absolutely essential communities talk with each other and plan ahead—and given the speed with which this is developing, they can't delay long," says Fearey.

WiFi Internet will open new possibilities—for example, log-in pages that serve as civic bulletin boards, fostering tighter-knit communities. But the most exciting vision yet comes from Cleveland, where Edward Hundert, Case Western's president, and Lev Gonick, the school's chief information officer, believe their OneCleveland technology and its Internet signal for thousands is just an enabler of something far broader. With all of Cleveland and Northeast Ohio in their sights, they want to create a national model of applying WiFi technology to bolster culture, advance learning, better health services and spread economic opportunity to pockets of extreme poverty.

To model its approach, Case Western built an extensive public wireless system linking its campus and its University Circle neighbors, including the world-famous Cleveland Orchestra, the Cleveland Museum of Art, Institute of Music, Natural History Museum, Botanical Gardens and four dozen other cultural, research, health-care and government institutions. "Every coffee shop, museum space, park here is now wireless enabled," says Gonick, adding "we say it should be like the air you breathe—free and available everywhere."

Cleveland Mayor Jane Campbell has identified herself closely with the OneCleveland initiative, in which such major technology companies as Cisco and IBM are also significant players. But the challenge seems immense: the Census Bureau recently declared Cleveland the nation's most impoverished major city. Technology, notes Gonick, needs to be "not only an enabler but a transformative agent for a community very much on the edge, with a steep precipice below us."

The historic reality is that new technologies are like double-bladed knives cutting through history—their positive impacts (like television's amazing imaging revolution) are often offset by unanticipated drawbacks (like TV's social isolation and dumbing-down impacts).

But if area-wide WiFi telecommunications can deliver even a fraction of the benefits its advocates see—from democratized broadband Internet to economic openings for the poor to unleashing university skills for cities and regions—then there'll be a lot more to proclaim than its rock-bottom cost.

2

The Potential Benefits of Municipal Wi-Fi Are Overstated

David P. McClure

David P. McClure is president of the U.S. Internet Industry Association (USIIA), the North American trade association for Internet commerce, content, and connectivity.

Government agencies—rarely known for their efficiency or innovation—now seem determined to enter the telecommunications business. Officials in dozens of cities have declared that they can offer inexpensive wi-fi technology to their citizens. According to proponents, citywide wi-fi will enhance government services, attract tourists, aid businesses, and enable the poor to connect to the Internet. None of these assertions are based on fact. Building, operating, and maintaining a complicated citywide wi-fi system is expensive and takes considerable technical skill. In addition, citywide wi-fi is redundant in most urban areas where there are ample broadband choices offered by private telecom companies. Wireless technology is certainly revolutionary and, in the future, nearly all Internet connections will be wireless. But city government should stay out of the telecom business and allow the free market to offer competitively priced wi-fi access to American citizens.

More than two hundred cities across the United States are now in the process of considering, testing or building out municipal broadband networks, with the majority of these

David P. McClure, "Not in the Public Interest—The Myths of Municipal Wireless Networks," *New Millennium Research Council*, February 2005, pp. 1–5. Copyright © 2005 New Millennium Research Council. All rights reserved. Reproduced by permission.

based on low-cost wireless Wi-Fi "mesh" networks. From Chaska, MN to Atlanta, GA, local governments and media pundits are touting such networks as a means to bring broadband to markets that are presently underserved:

> "For all their high-tech prowess, America's communications companies aren't exactly racing to offer people high-speed Internet access. . . . But dozens of cities and towns across the country—from Chaska, MN, to Corpus Christi, TX—can't wait. If companies won't wire them up, they are doing it themselves."

Proponents of the networks promise to deliver an extensive list of benefits:

> "By making technology ubiquitous and seamless to the public, Wi-Fi brings important benefits to the community as a whole such as workforce development, educational enrichment, and bridging the digital divide," says Dr. Jabari Simama, Executive Director of the Atlanta Mayor's Office of Community Technology.

While almost any effort that leads to the faster deployment of high-speed, reliable and secure Internet connectivity is laudable, the experience with municipal Wi-Fi networks to date has been long on hyperbole and short on quantifiable data.

There are substantive issues related to the creation of municipal networks—economic issues, technical and spectrum issues, political issues and philosophical issues related to the impact of a government's use of tax subsidies to disrupt competitive markets.

None of these issues, however, can be clearly and objectively addressed unless and until we are able to clear away the misperceptions, misstatements and myths of municipal networks.

Media Misrepresentations

Before undertaking any assessment of the validity of municipal networking efforts, it is essential to first cut through the fog of poorly written, anti-business media reports regarding the implementation of municipal networks.

Cities are unable to show any realistic research data indicating how many people will use the service, whether they will pay for the service, or how the city will pay for the network if the plan doesn't pan out.

Here's the spin: municipal Wi-Fi networking is a widespread, growing, David versus Goliath effort to bring broadband connectivity to communities poorly served—if at all—by existing broadband providers. Impatient and frightened of being left behind in the information economy, these communities can build and operate their own networks at rates much lower than those offered by companies whose goal is to make a profit. Consumers will get free Internet access and it will cost the cities almost nothing.

The reality is very different:

- The communities seeking Wi-Fi networks are largely metropolitan areas with excellent broadband availability. Cerritos, California lies in the heart of the Los Angeles metro area and is well served both by cable and DSL. Chaska, Minnesota is a suburb of Minneapolis/St. Paul, one of the "most wired" cities in America. Philadelphia and Atlanta are also among the cities listed among the "most wired" in America. Other "underserved" markets considering networks include Dayton, Ohio, and New York City.

- There is no shortage of broadband in these cities, or in most of the rest of the country. FCC [Federal Communications Commission] data shows consistent and aggressive double-digit growth in broadband deployment nationwide with 94 percent of all zip codes and all 50 states reporting broadband availability in June of 2004. Costs are also falling, as cable and telephone companies begin to recover the more than $100 billion they have invested in broadband infrastructure. Most major providers offer service for under $30 per month, and some as low as $19.95 per month.

- Proponents of municipal Wi-Fi networks have been unable to provide a coherent list of the benefits taxpayers will receive for their investment. Though some have attempted to define benefits in simple and vague terms, they can provide no quantifiable cost/benefit analysis. There is no proven business model for such networks, and cities are unable to show any realistic research data indicating how many people will use the service, whether they will pay for the service, or how the city will pay for the network if the plan doesn't pan out.

Benefits Analysis

The issue of cost-to-benefits analysis is important, because there is already substantial data available from other technology and municipal projects. While it may be difficult to impossible to specify the benefits that will accrue to residents from municipal networks, it is possible to determine some of the benefits that will *not* be realized:

- *Networks will not close the digital divide.* "Digital divide" has become a catch-all phrase to loosely define a state in which some persons are disadvantaged in their ability to access technology to the same extent as other persons. But it is important to realize that whatever divide may exist in any community is not simply a lack of free broadband services. A digital divide can take many forms—economic, physical (e.g., disabled access to technology), age-centric or even cultural. Likewise, the existence of such a divide can be related to any combination of factors, including ability to purchase a computer or other access device; relative computer literacy; lack of technical support; or even cultural resistance to education. Free access to high-speed internet services—already available in every school and library in the nation—has not closed these divisions.

• *Networks will not enhance the business development environment.* Though this is often cited as a benefit, econometric data shows no specific link between broadband availability and economic development. This may be because any business in the United States that needs or wants broadband connectivity can already have it via existing telephony, cable, satellite, or wireless providers. But it is also related to the fact that connectivity alone does not create a significant impact on the core determinants of economic growth: an increase in employment, or an increase in the personal incomes of residents.

• *Networks will not increase tourism.* For many major metropolitan destinations, ubiquitous Wi-Fi is touted as a means to attract tourists and business travelers. But it is difficult to imagine how municipal networks could offer more than the broadband services already offered by most major hotel chains, airports and commercial hotspots, including McDonald's restaurants and coffee shops. It is also instructive to view the data on utilization of these existing services—even when offered for free, few people make use of them because they are insecure, inconvenient or unnecessary. There is no data showing that tourists prefer to travel to cities with wireless networks.

- *"Mixed Use" networks will not enable better municipal services.* This benefit is derived from the assumption that a public Wi-Fi network can also be used to benefit emergency services, utility services and other legitimate municipal services. But two key elements of the assumption are impossible to validate because they have never before been done: first, Wi-Fi technology has not been shown to be an effective method to provide uninterrupted service over a large area; and second, there is no evidence that consumer broadband applications and municipal applications can effectively and securely co-exist on a single network. Indeed, efforts to test municipal use of wireless networks have already encountered problems with interference from other devices utilizing the same frequency ranges, including mobile phones and microwave ovens.

- *Networks will not be economically self-sustaining.* Perhaps the most common benefit cited for municipal Wi-Fi networks is their low cost and economic sustainability. Cities are told that Wi-Fi networks cost little to set up or operate, and that revenues from business taxes, advertising or user subscriptions from out-of-town visitors will more than compensate for any operating costs. The assumption is that residents and the disadvantaged will benefit from a wonderful, ubiquitous and free broadband service paid for by someone else. Data to support this assumption, however, does not exist—there is little evidence that broadband networks can be operated without extensive, continued investment. And even less evidence that the victims of the scheme—those who are chosen to pay for the network in order to give it away to others—are willing to so easily part with their money.

It is within the realm of possibility that some tangible benefit may be found to municipal operation of a public Wi-Fi network. But since experience with such networks is virtually non-existent and with no data available to support existing benefits claims, any such claims should be labeled speculative at best and nonsensical at worst.

Marietta, Georgia spent more than $35 million operating its broadband network before selling it at a loss in 2004.

The Regulatory Response

While there may be no data to support a tangible benefit for taxpayers and ratepayers, there is ample evidence to support the perceived political benefits to those who promote and support the creation of such networks. There are likely a myriad of other agendas at work, including simple mayoral bragging rights:

"The other broadband providers might lose a few customers," says Brad Mayer, who manages Chaska's Wi-Fi network. Sprint, Qwest, independent broadband vendors and Time Warner Cable are among the town's vendors. "There's been a lot done with wireless, but less with Wi-Fi. We are our own guinea pig. I think it's going to be a great thing."

"We also believe offering this type of exciting, pioneering service will go a long way toward helping Dayton attract that 'creative class' of people who will help fuel our community's future success."

"Proponents say the system . . . will let Atlanta compete with cities traditionally viewed as more Wi-Fi friendly—like San Francisco and Seattle—attracting tech-savvy businesses, workers and tourists to the area who want to access the Internet and corporate intranets on the go."

Consultants to these cities gain lucrative contracts to plan and build the networks—contracts which are often let without competitive bidding by existing broadband vendors in the community.

There is also evidence that such municipal projects can result in disaster. While Wi-Fi networks are a recent phenomenon, there has been extensive experience with municipal broadband networks via cable and fiber. And the record there is sobering:

- Iowa Communications Network requires massive subsidies just to stay in business.

- California's CALNET system was nearly $20 million in debt when it was sold in 1998.

- Lebanon, Ohio originally projected its fiber network would cost $5 million to build. The build-out cost was actually $9 million, and the city has been forced to raise an additional $14.8 million to cover operating losses.

- Marietta, Georgia spent more than $35 million operating its broadband network before selling it at a loss in 2004.

In order to prevent such disasters, and to remain consistent with federal regulatory and court rulings that bar municipalities from competing with private enterprises, state legislatures are toughening their consumer protection laws. Fifteen states, including Texas and Pennsylvania, now have laws to protect against misuse of public funds for such projects, and other states are considering model language on this issue.

3

Wi-Fi Technology Is Beneficial to High School Administrators

Ron Schachter

Ron Schachter is a freelance writer based in Newton, Massachusetts.

Wireless technology is changing the way teachers and students interact in the classroom. In Canadian schools, handheld wireless computers are increasing productivity, enhancing the teaching process, and freeing staff from laborious administrative tasks. From chemistry class to coaching, teachers are finding that they can review student records, create presentations, browse calendars, and effortlessly perform dozens of administrative tasks utilizing wi-fi technology at school.

North Grenville District High School is located north of the border in Kemptville, Ontario, but by placing palm-One handheld wireless computers in the hands of its 35 teachers this school about 45 minutes south of the Canadian capital Ottawa has moved to the heart of a brave new world.

"We're the only school in our district—which consists of 22 secondary schools and 122 schools all together—where all of the staff have handhelds," says Principal Steve McLean, who adds that his may be the only school in Ontario, and, for that matter all of Canada, to be using handhelds across the board.

This fall, North Grenville High installed a new WiFi wireless network. And currently, the school is upgrading its palm-

One fleet to WiFi-enabled Tungsten C models and adding eSIS software from Media-X that will let teachers take attendance with a click.

North Grenville's approach to the mundane but complicated daily task of attendance taking is only the latest in North Grenville's effort to make teachers, administrators, and staff more productive by using handhelds. That process began under McLean's leadership three years ago.

"In Canada, they've certainly been a leader," says educational partner Steve Moretti, president of software maker Media-X in Ottawa. "They've seen what the technology could do, and they've stayed the course."

"It had been a long time since we invested educationally in teachers in a meaningful way, and I started to look at whether using handhelds could be valuable," McLean recalls. "It took me about a year to work through this with staff because I was [needlessly] concerned about using any budget that we had available on something our people weren't going to support."

Nevertheless, two years ago, McLean purchased a set of palmOne handhelds and a suite of software applications from Media-X that allows his teachers to do everything from keeping calendars and making to-do lists to creating lesson plans and assessing students' work. . . . And McLean has noticed a difference, from the chemistry lab to the playing field.

When McLean observes a class, he looks for 16 teaching competencies spread across five domains—from commitment to students and student learning to teaching practice to professional knowledge.

Instant Record Keeping

"A chemistry teacher can be chatting with students about concepts that are taking place in a lab," McLean says. "If during that discussion the student has demonstrated mastery of a particular concept, the teacher can plug in that information right there."

"I can also check competencies as I walk around the lab," notes chemistry teacher Derek Cole. "I mark them off, boom, boom, boom." That instant record keeping translates to more effective meetings with students, he adds. "You can have immediate conferences anywhere with students who ask, 'How am I doing?'"

New Assistant Principal Jill Pensa notes, "In my old school, you had to bring the students to the computer to have that conversation."

Physical education teacher Sean Kelly uses his handheld to assess his students according to rubrics for skills in various sports. He estimates that he saves a half hour for every skill set he evaluates, compared to the paper and pencil routine he used to go through.

Guidance counselor Anne Parry has to manage a different flood of information and uses the handheld as a day planner and "graffiti" board. "My brain cannot contain all that people throw at me," she explains. "I could be looking for a student in the hall, and a teacher will give me two additional referrals."

Parry also can view photographs downloaded from the student yearbook. "If I hear about a person in trouble emotionally, I would have a name, but now I also have a face," she says.

Analyzing and Evaluating

For his part, Principal McLean makes full use of the Media-X products ePrincipal, a program for analyzing student achievement, and mVal, a tool for evaluating his teaching staff. When McLean observes a class, he looks for 16 teaching competencies spread across five domains—from commitment to students and student learning to teaching practice to professional knowledge.

"By using mVal, I can have all of this information on my handheld, and I would be basically clicking whether the teacher was 'satisfactory,' 'not satisfactory,' 'good,' or 'exemplary,'" McLean says. He can check off the sources he's using for evidence, such as student notes or teacher lesson plans. The mVal program also stores his pre-conference observations and can download the teacher's self-evaluation for comparison with McLean's view of the situation.

"By comparison," McLean points out, "some of my colleagues in other schools who are less comfortable using the technology, would go in and sit at the back of the classroom in typical fashion with a pad of paper, scribble down notes, then come back to the office at a later time and have to input all the data, sort it all out, and develop the appraisal document. I, on the other hand, come back to my office and synchronize my handheld. And eventually, with the WiFi network, I won't even have to perform a HotSync operation because it will be able to be done wirelessly from any classroom on campus."

McLean estimates that in the past, he's spent 20 to 40 hours, twice a year, for each teacher's evaluation. "It's an incredibly powerful program," he says. "It's made my practice easier, and it's a huge timesaver. It cuts my time in half."

Taming Attendance

What's currently causing the biggest stir at North Grenville, though, is the immediate prospect of bringing an unwieldy attendance system under control, a transformation that received a boost when a local Internet provider installed a new WiFi network for free.

"I have secretarial staff who are very talented, resourceful people and right now we're wasting talent and resources because we're underutilizing them," says McLean. "One of my staff members sits all day and collects these sheets of paper, and she inputs attendance all day. It's a terrible waste of her talent when a teacher could actually click off attendance on a handheld."

We're all going to be on the same page. We're all going to be linked. I think we will have a united front.

That staff member is Pat Johnston, who every day has to wait on four sets of class attendance sheets from each teacher. "Teachers lose their sheets or hand them in late," she says, adding that it's anybody's guess when she will get an accurate count.

"Sometimes I get the attendance by the end of class, sometimes by noon, sometimes by the end of the day," Johnston says. "If a mother calls at 9 and says, 'Is Johnny there?', I may not be able to answer her. If the teachers have done the attendance on their handhelds, I'll be able to know where the students are right on the spot."

Besides the more accurate and immediate reporting, the new system will free up Johnston to follow up on missing students by calling home and by providing what McLean sees as more useful record keeping.

"As in the United States, we're becoming cognizant of the need for good data and how to turn that data into useful information," he says. He's also looking forward to installing iNotice software from Media-X, which enables users to contact parents by email from anywhere in the building.

"For example," says McLean, "every month, my staff have been making what we call 'good news' phone calls, where you call home and say, 'I caught Johnny being good.' iNotice allows staff to send messages by email right then and there, on the spot."

"It not only lets you record student achievements, you can record other incidents you might not ordinarily record and put them in a central database," adds Media-X's Moretti.

"People are more likely to seize the moment because the handheld is so easy to use. What seem like minor incidents can add up, and the product is pretty powerful."

Those contacts are part of Ontario's requirement that teachers get in touch with parents regularly. By using palmOne handhelds, McLean says, the school will better be able to document and correlate these efforts.

All this progress with handhelds has the North Grenville staff imagining the possibilities down the line. "We're all going to be on the same page," predicts Parry. "We're all going to be linked. I think we will have a united front."

"I coach the school basketball team," says physical education teacher Kelly, "and Derek coaches the cross-country team. And there are a number of sport management applications for palmOne handhelds for charting a basketball game, or for keeping times at a cross-country meet, or keeping statistics in volleyball or hockey.

"If we could integrate that software, we could eliminate a lot of paperwork for all of our coaches, and we could give instantaneous feedback at halftime or in between periods or in the middle of a meet on how the athletes are doing. If somehow it were possible financially, it would be another convenience, another efficiency."

Handhelds Ahead

In the meantime, other schools in the district have expressed interest in North Grenville's widespread use of handheld technology. McLean discovered mVal on his own and has since conducted training sessions with other schools. Last year the entire district adopted that application for staff evaluations.

"I always get the questions of, 'How did you do that?'" says McLean. His answer: time, energy, and forging partnerships. "I share with my colleagues because I think that's part of my role as well," he says. "If it's good for North Grenville, chances are it will be good for South Grenville and Brockville Collegiate and other schools in our district."

"That's very elite company in terms of our thinking and embracing of technology," McLean says. He credits his staff, but he also recalls what it was like before he began using his handheld computer almost four years ago. He depended on an appointment book to get him through the school day.

"I was quite a disciple of the old Day-Timer," he says. "It contained my contacts, my appointments, my to-do list. It was the printed version of a handheld. My secretary would make appointments for me. I would be out of the school, and I would make appointments for me. But they would never, ever get into my book."

McLean made a one-week transition to using the hand-held. "It was easy, and I stopped carrying my appointment book a week later. I stopped being late for meetings. I'd be driving to wherever I was going, without knowing how to get there, but it was now in the handheld."

McLean and his staff have come much further down the road, with palmOne handhelds as their primary vehicle. "If we're spending less time on the 'administrivia' end of things," he adds, "then there's more time and energy going into teaching and learning and student achievement."

4

Wireless Classrooms Present Many Challenges to Teachers

Mahesh P. Bhave

Mahesh P. Bhave is vice president of new business development for Hughes Network Systems Inc. in San Diego, California.

Wireless technology is transforming the way students perform their work at school, but the changes are creating new challenges for teachers. With laptop computers working on wireless net works, students can take notes and access Web sites pertinent to the lesson. However, students can also ignore the teacher while playing video games, sending instant messages, surfing the Web, or reading e-mail. Laptops may also allow students to cheat on tests. Although classroom Web surfing is an inevitable outgrowth of the wi-fi revolution, teachers need to limit access in order to maintain control over students.

Wi-fi technologies will soon permeate classrooms in schools and colleges just as they have started to enter business conference rooms. When they do, they will raise issues of stewardship and control for teachers. How can a teacher assert the necessary and traditional control over classroom proceedings to remain effective? How can a teacher retain focus and discipline in the classroom when students multitask with ease? Can the technologies be used for educational benefits, e.g., through augmenting subject matter with instant research or through greater participation? This article will try to address some of the behavioral issues that emerge when Wi-Fi access becomes commonplace in the classroom.

Graduate seminar rooms and lecture halls are equipped, or can be readily furnished, with projectors, screens and whiteboards, while phone lines typically link these rooms to the outside world, both for voice and dial-up data services. However, Wi-Fi in such settings is new and growing, and the behaviors of business people in these settings offer insights into what can be expected in the classroom. Already, a number of colleges have some form of wireless connectivity on campus, including Dartmouth College [in New Hampshire] and Franklin & Marshall College in Pennsylvania. In secondary education, the Maine Learning Technology Initiative is introducing laptops for all 17,000 of the state's seventh-graders as an experiment [in 2002]. In addition, many other school districts nationwide are implementing smaller wireless programs.

As laptop use spreads among students, its use will extend outside of the classroom and into places such as bookstore cafes, lounges and homes. The technologies clearly represent an intervention in the classroom and a pedagogical challenge. Classroom etiquette may change; and learning potential may increase through healthy, intraclassroom, nondisruptive communications, as well as through the use of the Internet's timely, global resources.

Revolutions in the Classroom

[In 1995] I witnessed the combined wireless and portable Internet revolutions. Auctions of PCS (personal communications services) frequency by the Federal Communications Commission had launched the digital wireless voice revolution, and the Mosaic browser had launched the Internet revolution. I concluded that student and teacher behavior in Wi-Fi-enhanced classrooms would materially change, because there would be new options for interaction between:

- Students among themselves;

- Students with their teachers;

- Students with outsiders; and

- Students and teachers with the Internet.

These new options would prove to be beneficial to the class at times and disadvantageous to the class at other times. Regardless, I concluded that the presence of people outside of the classroom and the variety of knowledge on the Internet would inevitably permeate the classroom even while in session.

Browsing, playing computer games, exchanging e-mail and Internet messaging might substitute for doodling.

Understanding New Behaviors

The principal argument of this paper is that the coexistence and interworking of several factors in the classroom's limited space is central to the understanding of new behaviors, not any technologies per se. The "presence in a context," or agglomeration, principally determines behavioral change. Therefore, you have to take into account the availability of laptops in critical numbers, their ability to network with each other and the Internet, and their convenient wireless use. Also, you have to consider the topology of the room and the interplay of these technologies with the existing technologies, such as a projector or whiteboard.

In classrooms today, the whiteboard and the projector live an uneasy coexistence. When the two are on the same wall, and the projection screen has to move up before the whiteboard can be used, a clumsy procedure results. Moving the projector screen to the side or having the whiteboard moved to other walls can redress this issue. However, when both the projection screen and the whiteboard are needed, the focus of the room shifts from wall to screen and vice versa. This means students' chairs turn and the educator's position of control is compromised.

Then, there are the issues of control and focus due to the relative placement of the whiteboard and projector when many participants have laptops wirelessly connected to the Internet and intranet. The students are therefore linked to the outside world even as they participate in class. Unlike whispering or passing paper notes, the students can nondisruptively communicate with each other through the access point, as well as in a peer-to-peer manner.

In the future, when the projector is an element on the wireless network, anyone in the classroom can control the projected contents wirelessly, mediated through a suitable user interface available for each participant, but controlled in a "master" fashion by the educator. The presence of laptops and Wi-Fi thus creates an extremely open environment thereby exacerbating the problem of an educator's control. In addition to issues of student discipline and attentiveness, the increasing use of the projector alongside the whiteboard in their varying topologies already challenges a teacher's control. This challenge to control is exacerbated by the presence of wirelessly connected laptops.

Classroom Dynamics with Wireless Internet

Laptops will enter classrooms as substitutes for traditional notebook folders, whether or not they have any other educational benefit, and whether or not they are connected to the Internet. However, when connected, there will be an electronic dialogue in class among students and with the outside world even as the teacher is talking. The normal "one-to-many" method of any teacher will now be augmented and overlaid by numerous one-to-many electronic conversations, messages and alerts from the outside.

Browsing, playing computer games, exchanging e-mail and Internet messaging might substitute for doodling. Such exchanges may not be easily controlled or stopped by a teacher in the interest of better classroom participation. It would look normal enough, no more or less than note taking. Students paying attention in class would be indistinguishable from those who are not, though the body language will remain the same. Several novel issues arise as a result:

- Should eye contact remain as important in this new environment?

- Should laptops be allowed during exams and quizzes?

- Do Wi-Fi-enhanced classrooms create a new teaching format?

- Does a question asked electronically have lower priority than a student's raised hand?

- What happens to participation when note taking is less [like] transcribing what is presented and more like annotation?

- How does the classroom dynamic change when what is on the board is also simultaneously on students' screens?

Controlling Classroom Content and Agenda

Just what the new protocols for control and discipline will be is difficult to predict. Some possibilities include:

- No laptops allowed in the room. The laptop as a substitute for a notebook folder will be difficult to prohibit. Calculators were once prohibited in the belief that their use would impair students' computational abilities.

- Laptops allowed for taking notes, for local content, but no access to the Internet (or enterprise LAN) in the classroom. This too would be difficult to implement given that Wi-Fi functionalities will be embedded in laptops, and PC cards for mobile data services will either be embedded or have small form factors.

- Laptops allowed, access to enterprise LAN and the Internet permitted, and, with the teacher's permission, can be used to augment learning. The contents from the Internet may be shared with the group or projected for discussion. This will be the norm, I suspect, and some kind of honor code will prevail so that its use will be judicious and respectful of others.

Apart from the do's and don'ts in a classroom, which are the prerogatives of the teacher, it is possible to have a limited technical solution to the problem of metering and regulating access to outside content during class. A "master" computer belonging to the teacher can control the access point (AP) that is feeding the classroom. At different times during the class, the AP may be "opened" to various degrees by the teacher. For example, the teacher may allow "one-to-many" access—only the instructor can send information to the class through the AP. Such a solution may be implemented through specialized or proprietary APs specifically designed for classrooms.

When integrated with projectors, whiteboards and connectivity, laptops can be considered a disruptive technology.

On occasions, when research requires access to the Internet for each student, the teacher may switch the AP to an "Open" or "Internet" mode. Once the research is done, say after 15 minutes, the teacher can switch off the Internet connection. This may be reasonable; yet it may not be enforceable. This is because the coverage from mobile carriers could encompass classrooms, and any student who wishes may access the Internet regardless of the teacher's controls. Control over Internet access would therefore have to be exercised through subscription management by parents.

Laptops can be used for note taking, but unlike traditional notebooks, they open vertically. Such open flaps of laptop screens have the potential of becoming a mild irritant in the classroom. Whereas open laptop screens on the same side of the table are collaborative, when across the table they can be unintentionally rude. Laptops also allow students to hide behind the open screen and avoid teacher eye contact. Emerging etiquette may require that only screens of a certain size be appropriate for classrooms or meetings, or that they be folded down sufficiently. This raises all kinds of product design and ergonomics issues—readability, footprint or projection on the table, space needed per person, body posture, etc. To my knowledge, no notebook computer opens on the side of the keyboard, functioning as a true notebook. Tablet PCs may offset this limitation, but their acceptability remains to be established.

A Permeable Classroom

Wi-Fi technologies have flooded classrooms with no sign of letting up. They pose challenges to teachers' classroom objectives, require new etiquette and protocols for control, and have the potential to enhance learning. Conducting trials in actual classrooms appears to be the best way to learn how behavior will be shaped. . . . But many more studies with specific behavioral and ergonomic objectives are necessary; particularly those focused on the interplay of the technologies with their context.

Phones, smart phones and connected PDAs have already rendered the classroom permeable to outside interruptions. Connected laptops or notebook computers, however, qualitatively change the environment since they are legitimate tools for the classroom. Simpler protocols, such as requiring students to turn off their phones or set them to vibrate mode, are no longer sufficient. When integrated with projectors, whiteboards and connectivity, laptops can be considered a disruptive technology.

Such disruption can be in the service of superior learning. But the teacher must first learn to harness them, in addition to controlling them, for extracting benefits. This also needs to be determined through well-defined trials. If such disruptive technologies do indeed enhance learning, its absence in certain schools represents deprivation, and it potentially adds to the digital divide. The Maine schools solved the problem of iniquitous access by giving all middle school students a state-issued laptop. But this might well be only an interim solution.

More likely, schools will be permanently Wi-Fi enabled as a campus and students will have a choice in their use of laptops. Such a choice of laptops purchased as part of school supplies is the more likely future, and such choices are more of the "American Way" than the Maine solution. After all, the laptop is a personal utility terminal outside of the classroom. Just as one may perceive the classroom boundaries to have been breached, it is also now possible to say that learning opportunities have expanded beyond the classroom to include any small conference table where students can gather and collaboratively do research and work.

It's now possible for a student to be sick at home, while still being able to participate in class. Not merely by teleconferencing or videoconferencing, which is stilted and can be disruptive, but by merely linking into the projector and camera in the classroom from anywhere in the world. This represents a kind of ad hoc, online, distance learning, except that instead of the teacher's presence radiating out to classrooms across geography, the student zooms into the classroom. Such a classroom is potentially even more "open" than what Wi-Fi achieves inside the class. It is not clear when the effectiveness of a teacher breaks down, and when learning impaired options for instructional design are as wide open as this. Determining such limits to openness is also an area for future research. Until the impact from these new technologies stabilizes, the teacher needs to draw the line at what is permissible, no matter what is possible.

5

Wireless Technology Boosts Business Productivity

Intel Information Technology

Intel is a multinational corporation best known for designing and manufacturing microprocessors and specialized integrated circuits.

Wi-fi technology provides many benefits in the work environment. The costs of installing wireless networks are about half that of installing wired connections. In addition, wi-fi networks measurably improve worker efficiency and have a positive impact on work quality. By using wi-fi workers are saving almost one hour a week through multitasking at meetings. Wireless technology also allows employees to arrange spontaneous meetings and even work from home. With this new technology, the costs of doing business drops while worker morale improves along with output.

This study expands previous research by ... examining the impact of wireless technology on office worker behavior.

We particularly focused on measuring the impact of wireless connectivity in meetings and how that impacts productivity. Although Intel already supports wired network access during meetings in many locations, such as conference rooms, each location has only so many wired network ports, which limits the number of wired users. Wireless can host a higher number of users and allows those users greater flexibility.

The Intel IT Business Value Program performed a study to establish whether wireless technology had quantifiable benefits over wired technology for office workers. Our goal for this study was to understand the value of wireless in a business environment.

We first tried to determine whether wireless network access had any advantages over wired access in meetings. More specifically, we wanted to determine if wireless users were able to do more multitasking in meetings, away from their desk, than wired users. We also examined users' comments and survey data to better understand the impact of using wireless at home and to gather additional insights on the benefits of using wireless. . . .

Our study showed that use of wireless access influences user behavior. . . .

We found that wireless users brought their notebooks to meetings 16 percent more often than did wired users, 84 percent for wireless users as compared to 68 percent for wired users. These results were statistically significant. . . .

Our interpretation, based on user comments, is that this was partly due to the convenience of avoiding cables and connection ports and partly due to the fact that users can connect in meeting areas that they could not have connected in previously, such as conference rooms that are full or the cafeterias that have only wireless network access.

Interestingly, the comments from our wired users who wish they had wireless also supported this finding. 3 percent of our wired user comments indicated that if they had wireless that they would bring their notebooks to meetings more often.

The Ability to Successfully Connect

We asked users how many meetings they wanted to connect in and how many of those meetings they were successfully able to connect in. We then calculated the percentage of meetings where wireless and wired users were able to connect successfully. We found that wireless access users were able to connect successfully more often than wired users. . . .

It's generally easier to provide wireless access than wired access. For one thing, while it's difficult to anticipate how many wired ports you need in a location, wireless service is more elastic. Plus, wireless access is less expensive. Intel IT estimates that it costs about half as much to wire a 3,000 employee building with wireless as compared to wired, about 1 million dollars as compared to about 2 million dollars. We also estimate that maintenance costs of a wireless network are less than for a wired network.

With more wireless users bringing their notebooks to meetings and successfully connecting to the network, we expect that more wireless users would multitask during meetings. These users would realize the benefits of multitasking.

Time and Money Savings

Our data shows that wireless users performed network connected activities in meetings 368 minutes per week as compared to 316 minutes per week for wired users. Wireless users were able to complete 52 more minutes per week of connected activities during meetings than wired users, thereby increasing their productivity. . . .

We evaluated the financial impact of the productivity improvements due to wireless for office workers by looking at the cost of each employee's time. . . .

The 52 minutes per week represents a productivity improvement of approximately 2.17 percent, or about 41.6 hours per year. So for example, a company with 25,000 employees and a per-employee total cost/burden rate of $50 per hour would realize approximately $52,000,000. However when estimating these types of benefits as part of the IT Business Value program, we discount the dollar amount by 50 percent. So the benefit after the 50 percent discount would be $26,000,000.

Of course all corporations will be different. Some corporations may have a culture that prevents a change in behavior of taking notebooks to multitask in meetings or they may have meetings where the user must devote full attention to all aspects of the meeting, limiting any type of multitasking. Other companies may not have the same need as Intel to be connected to the network in meetings. In other cases, companies may have no previous wired infrastructure in meeting areas. All of these factors could alter any benefit. We believe that any multitasking strategy in meetings should be done intelligently, in a manner that will strengthen the impact of what needs to be accomplished in a meeting rather than detracting from it.

Further Benefits of Wireless

In addition to the quantifiable benefits listed above, comments from the wireless users helped us identify other benefits that we could not measure. These include additional benefits of multitasking in meetings, spontaneous collaborative meetings, and wireless at home.

Wireless user comments indicated that wireless connectivity allows greater flexibility to connect to the network at work. In fact 47 percent of the wireless users in our study reported that greater flexibility was a key benefit of wireless over wired network connections. For example, because of a limited number of conference rooms, Intel employees use the cafeteria to hold meetings. In response, we installed wireless access points in Intel cafeterias to provide network access, and now employees can gather there or at some other isolated location that does not have any wired network connections and still be connected to the network.

One factor that may contribute to this flexibility is greater ease of connectivity—14 percent of wireless user comments indicated that they liked the fact that they did not have to carry network cables or dongles around with them, and 16 percent of our wireless users stated that wireless made it quicker and easier to connect to the network.

Multitasking During Meetings

Our wireless users were able to multitask in meetings 52 minutes more per week than wired users. Aside from the productivity benefit, what additional benefits might there be? We suggest that it enabled more of the same kinds of benefits that being connected in meetings in general enables.

Being connected to the network in meetings enables workers to:

- *Gather required information from outside the meeting.* 38 percent of our wireless user comments indicated that their wireless gave them access to information outside of the meeting. User comments indicated that this helps them answer questions, make decisions faster, and speeds up the overall process of getting things done. This is especially apparent in meetings in places like the cafeteria where no other network connectivity is available.

"[Wireless enables me to] bring my notebook everywhere I go with full data availability."

- *Share information with meeting members more easily.* 28 percent of our wireless users indicated that sharing data or presentations with other meeting members was enhanced by their ability to connect wirelessly in meetings. For example:

"In one conference room, the hub was not working. Only wireless notebook users were able to connect to [our data sharing application]."

"We were not able to reserve a notebook projector for our meeting, but we were able to all sit in a conference room and share a presentation over the [data sharing application], thanks to wireless!"

- *Use meeting time more efficiently.* For example, people who have several meetings in a row in the cafeteria can now be more productive in-between meetings because wireless enables them to stay connected and get more done. 14 percent of wireless users expressed how wireless enabled them to make better use of their time in meetings. 41 percent mentioned how they could take care of additional meeting scheduling or other meeting related activities during the meeting instead of having to follow up after the meeting.

"Online in a common area—can't do that wired! Made better use of time between [meetings] in our cafeteria."

Wireless enables users to be connected to the network more, providing a greater opportunity to take advantage of the benefits of network connectivity in meetings.

Spontaneous Wireless Collaborative Meetings

Spontaneous wireless meetings occur when a wireless user takes their notebook to another person's cubicle or to another common area like the cafeteria to collaborate. These spontaneous meetings are a wireless benefit because they occur in places where wireless offers the only method of connecting to the network. Our user comments indicate that spontaneous meetings have significant benefit. Just over 9 percent of our wireless user comments indicated that spontaneous meetings are a significant wireless benefit.

"Wireless makes it very easy to move around the building from meeting to meeting or to [hold] spontaneous meetings and still have full access to design data and applications."

For example, a spontaneous meeting to discuss a design problem that is facilitated by bringing a wireless notebook to another worker's office can quickly and effectively resolve a problem.

4 percent of our wireless users mentioned that wireless enabled them to respond to important situations more quickly. Wireless workers can be connected a higher percentage of the time in meetings or in other locations and be more available to respond to important situations.

When I work from home, I use Wi-Fi so I can be anywhere in my house and work. If I didn't have Wi-Fi, I would probably work from home a lot less.

Wireless at Home

Of those who use wireless at work, 66 percent also have wireless networks at home. 36 percent of those who have wireless at home expressed how wireless at home gave them greater flexibility. User comments indicated that this flexibility included being able to work in a quieter location, a more comfortable location, a more enjoyable location. It also included being able to multitask with home activities like watching the kids.

This flexibility also helped some people keep up with heavy workloads. It enabled some people to work from home in spite of competing factors that would have otherwise prevented it. For example:

> "When I work from home, I use Wi-Fi so I can be anywhere in my house and work. If I didn't have Wi-Fi, I would probably work from home a lot less."

Wireless users also perceived that wireless helped them be more productive. In our survey, 93 percent of wireless users believed that their network connection at home made them more productive, compared to 78 percent of broadband wired users and only 21 percent of dial-up users. . . .

We found ways to demonstrate that wireless technology can measurably improve worker productivity, which participant comments indicate may lead to faster problem solving and answers to questions. We found other benefits through using wireless in spontaneous collaborative meetings and work and greater flexibility and productivity at home. Of course, the benefit that organizations receive from wireless will differ. The organizations that can benefit most have high collaboration needs, where fast access to information and rapid decision making are important.

6

Wireless Networks Can Have Negative Consequences for Employees

Jyoti Thottam

Jyoti Thottam is a writer living in Brooklyn and is a past president of the South Asian Journalists' Association.

Wi-fi technology ostensibly enables companies to wring more efficiency from their workers, but the increased output comes at a cost. With wireless connections at work, home, and in airports and hotels, employees are finding that they can never truly get away from the office. Even at work, wi-fi laptop use at meetings is proving to be a major distraction. Although there are many benefits to wireless technology, its use and overuse can have negative consequences as well.

What if you could work online from anywhere, inside your office or out? Check e-mail in the conference room, submit an expense report while waiting for a delayed flight, instant message from a coffee shop. With no more walls to demarcate your work space, would you be more productive, or just worn out?

That's exactly what the employees at iAnywhere Solutions, a unit of Sybase headquartered in Waterloo, Ontario, are trying to figure out. About 18 months ago the company, which makes software for handheld devices, plunged headlong into the wireless world by turning its entire campus into a giant wi-fi hot spot. Employees—mostly in marketing and product development—with wi-fi-enabled laptops (about half the 250 full-time staff at headquarters) can access the Web at lightning speed from anywhere in the building, no wires necessary.

What's so great about wi-fi that a company would reconfigure its entire computer infrastructure around it? For openers, it's as fast as a high-speed T1 line, more convenient than a mobile phone, as addictive as a BlackBerry and nearly imperceptible. What's not so great about it? Same thing. Wi-fi makes work that much easier to do and that much harder to escape. "We're just adapting to this new environment, adapting to what the technology allows you to do," says Martyn Mallick, a product manager at iAnywhere.

Sometimes I find it distracting . . . when I'm giving a presentation, and everyone's typing away on their laptops.

The company is one of a surprisingly small number of U.S. firms that have installed wi-fi networks. Fewer than 5% of U.S. workers [used them in 2003], according to an estimate by Gartner, a high-tech research firm. With IT [information technology] budgets squeezed, few companies are rolling out new projects that don't immediately add to the bottom line. But pioneers like iAnywhere are giving it a shot—and giving the rest of us a preview of what the wireless workplace is like.

So far, the biggest change has been felt in meetings, which used to be decidedly low-tech. Employees used to jot notes in black, spiral-bound paper notebooks and later transfer the most important information to their computers. Now they're toting around laptops, and instead of just taking notes at meetings, Mallick and his colleagues are exchanging files, looking up stuff on the Web—a description of a competitor's product, for instance—and consulting their calendars to choose a time for their next meeting. "Before, everyone would leave, and maybe 13 e-mails would go around," Mallick says. By dealing with questions as they arise, staff members can move on "action items" as they pop up. "Sometimes I would come out of a meeting with a page or two of things to do," says Milja Gillespie, a marketing manager at iAnywhere. "I can easily cut that in half."

Mallick admits, however, that attending a meeting full of people communing with their laptops instead of one another can be strange. "Sometimes I find it distracting," he says, "when I'm giving a presentation, and everyone's typing away on their laptops. It's a bit of a mind-set change, that people are actually working, that this is the new workplace." It isn't too hard to tell, though, when people are goofing off. "If they are looking up and paying attention to you and making eye contact, their body language tells a lot about whether they're part of a meeting."

At some companies, says Gartner wireless analyst Phillip Redman, the wi-fi distractions at meetings have got so bad that they use the "say the name twice" rule, because that's often what it takes to get someone's attention.

Because wi-fi makes it so easy to jump on the corporate network from your living room, more employees are working longer hours.

In a way, this is similar to the adjustment people went through with cell phones and BlackBerries: a period of intense use (and overuse) followed by a mellowing out as new ground rules emerge. Gillespie, for example, says she leaves her laptop on her desk when she and her colleagues are brainstorming. And Mallick says certain tasks require the focused concentration an old-fashioned desk provides. "I don't find I can do software development in an airport," he says.

And, to be sure, wi-fi doesn't make sense for every employee. iAnywhere didn't try to replace its wired network entirely, says CEO Terry Stepien. Some of its engineers need even more bandwidth than the fastest wi-fi networks can support, and the tech-support staff need desks with phone lines, so they don't use wireless laptops. (Eventually, some of them will be able to work wirelessly, using an Internet phone system instead of a regular phone.)

Perhaps the true promise (or hazard) of wi-fi for business, says Gartner analyst Leslie Fiering, is its use as a "day extender"—as yet another way to bring work home. Fiering estimates that wi-fi raises the per-employee cost of a laptop by as much as 4% a year, about $325, depending largely on wi-fi access charges while traveling.

Some of that cost is justified by employees' improved productivity on the road. "I'm no longer a bottleneck [when traveling]," Gillespie says. Mallick says he doesn't even set his out-of-office message anymore for short trips. For well-paid knowledge workers, the cost of wi-fi is even more readily absorbed by the extra time they willingly spend on work at home. Because wi-fi makes it so easy to jump on the corporate network from your living room, more employees are working longer hours. Mallick, for instance, says that since he got wi-fi installed at home he works about 10 hours more every week—and that's down from 15 when wi-fi first arrived. "I don't find it that inconvenient to sit on my couch and pull out my laptop," he says. That's good for work, but how good is it for his home life? "It mostly comes down to willpower," Mallick says. "There are times when I say, 'Ugh, why am I doing this?'" While iAnywhere hasn't clipped its wires entirely, that may be an option for smaller firms. Gartner's Fiering says she expects significant growth in corporate wireless networks to come from small companies that use wi-fi to avoid altogether the expensive investment in cabling. That allows them to move offices quickly when they outgrow them or when their rent goes up.

Perhaps the most intriguing promise of the wireless work-place is that it could allow offices to be more like they used to be. All that wiring has been shaping the way offices look—in some buildings, for example, walls are built not to support the structure but to carry cabling. Next year iAnywhere will move into a brand-new space on the campus of the University of Waterloo that has been conceived with wi-fi in mind. Patrick Simmons, a partner in the firm designing the building, RHL Architects, says wi-fi removes constraints that have become second nature to architects. "You were kind of tethered to the system," Simmons says. "[With wi-fi], you don't have to have walls in a certain place, have dropped ceilings just to give you access to cabling. You don't have to group people within certain distances of server rooms."

7

Using a Wi-Fi Network Poses Security Risks

Stephen Lawson

Stephen Lawson is a technology reporter for the IDG News Service.

Wi-fi networks enable users to easily log onto the Internet but this technology also enables hackers to steal passwords, files, and e-mail from innocent users. This information may be modified, posted on the Internet, or used for criminal purposes. Hackers may also use an unguarded wi-fi connection to turn an unsuspecting individual's computer into a "bot" that spreads viruses or malicious codes. Although precautions may be taken to prevent these problems, many people are either unaware that they need to take steps or forgetful when it comes to instituting preventive security measures. Whenever a new technology is introduced, criminals will find a way to use it for their own ends. Those who use wi-fi for its convenience should be aware of the security risks and take steps to protect themselves.

Benjamin Smith III and Gregory Straszkiewicz both were arrested for allegedly stealing something no one could see, hear or feel. That thing was valuable enough for victims to press charges in both cases. But the arrests were over something many consumers throw out their windows every day: a Wi-Fi signal.

The idea of a police car roaring down the street to catch a roving "Doom" junkie using someone else's wireless LAN [lo-

Stephen Lawson, "The Case of the Stolen Wi-Fi: What You Need to Know," *InfoWorld* August 8, 2005. Copyright © 2006 IDG Network. Republished with permission of InfoWorld, conveyed through Copyright Clearance Center, Inc.

cal area network] may seem silly, but there are real dangers if your network plays host to strangers. The hazards you might face include eavesdropping, theft of data, painful legal hassles or even a conviction for computer-related crimes. And if you casually tap into your neighbor's Wi-Fi sometimes, these arrests—Smith's in Florida and Straszkiewicz's in Isleworth, U.K.—signal that it's at least possible you might run afoul of a law and an irritated fellow citizen.

Charged with a Felony

On April 21, [2005,] Richard Dinon of St. Petersburg, Florida, called police after he saw Smith in a car on the street outside his house using a notebook computer. Smith, 40, was arrested and charged with a felony under a Florida law that prohibits unauthorized access to a computer or network, according to police. . . . In July [2005], a court in Isleworth convicted Straszkiewicz of using a laptop to access the Internet over unprotected residential wireless LANs on several occasions. He was fined 500 pounds (US $874 at the time) and got a 12-month conditional discharge.

People who steal bandwidth aren't necessarily going to stop there; they might steal data as well.

A typical home Wi-Fi signal can transmit about 150 feet (46 meters) from an access point or router. Walls and windows will slow it down, but if it reaches the edge of your property, it won't stop there. In densely populated areas, it's common for a Wi-Fi device such as a notebook to detect multiple residential networks from one place.

It's not hard for even an innocent user to tap into a broadband Internet connection via an unprotected wireless LAN: As soon as the Wi-Fi client detects the network, the user can click on it and join. Some broadband subscribers even like opening their networks. But Internet access may not be the only thing being shared.

"People who steal bandwidth aren't necessarily going to stop there; they might steal data as well," said Gartner Inc. analyst Richard Hunter. Most consumers wouldn't even know if a stranger was using the network, he added.

"If you've got an unprotected Wi-Fi network and you are in any kind of populated area, then you really should do something to protect that," Hunter said.

Specifically, on a Windows PC, an intruder on your wireless LAN could get into any folder that is set with file sharing enabled, Hunter said. Whatever is in the file could be modified, copied or posted on the Internet. So whatever you do, file sharing should be disabled, or restricted to certain trusted people on every folder, he said. That would at least prevent "a very casual hacker" from snooping in your files, Hunter said. File sharing is enabled by default in Windows XP Home Edition, according to Microsoft.

If you instruct your browser to save your passwords, an intruder might be able to steal them from your PC.

Likewise, it wouldn't be hard for someone to monitor data being sent from that unprotected LAN out to the Internet, said Kevin Bankston, an attorney at the Electronic Frontier Foundation. That could include e-mail messages and passwords. Even a low-priority password such as one for a free news site could pose a hazard for a user who sets up the same password on high-priority sites, Bankston pointed out. For users of unprotected Wi-Fi networks, he recommends encrypting e-mail and passwords with a tool such as Pretty Good Privacy (PGP) freeware.

Viruses and Malicious Codes

Having an open wireless LAN also could make you more vulnerable to viruses and other malicious codes, according to security experts. The biggest danger in that respect comes from users who just want to share an Internet connection, said Gartner security analyst John Girard. Many home Wi-Fi routers are equipped with firewalls, which can provide protections such as deflecting attempts to scan your PC for vulnerabilities. Anyone who gets on your wireless LAN is behind the firewall, so if their systems are laden with viruses or other malicious code it can spread over the LAN. This includes tools that search for systems to turn into "bots" controlled by hackers.

One area where wireless LAN users have less to worry about is interception of online passwords, said Martin Herfurt, founder of Trifinite Group, a group of European wireless security experts. Internet commerce sites that secure customer transactions will encrypt passwords and other information all the way from the user's browser to the store's server, so the same protections are there on the LAN as on the Internet, he said. However, if you instruct your browser to save your passwords, an intruder might be able to steal them from your PC, he added. In addition, some kinds of Internet-borne attacks let hackers record your keystrokes, according to Gartner's Girard. For the best protection, he recommends having firewalls in both the router and PC.

A Link to Crime

Though it's less likely, an intruder could cause serious problems even without getting into your computer. Whatever that person did over your Internet connection—which could include downloading child porn, sharing copyrighted content, or executing a denial-of-service attack—could be linked to you, observers said.

When crimes are suspected on the Internet, usually the first piece of evidence investigators look for is the IP (Internet Protocol) address from which the activity was carried out, the EFF's Bankston said. Organizations such as the Federal Bureau of Investigation or the Recording Industry Association of America can subpoena your Internet service provider to find out who you are.

Though there aren't many precedents from which to judge, lacking any other evidence, it's unlikely someone with an unprotected Wi-Fi network would be convicted just because a crime was committed from that network, both Hunter and Bankston said. But along the way, investigators could seize your computer to look for evidence and discover something else that could get you in trouble, such as your own illegally downloaded music, he said.

For that matter, arrests for "stealing" Wi-Fi are still rare and if someone taps into your network, in some places it may be hard to prosecute them, Bankston said. It's hard to prove an intruder was deliberately snooping rather than just taking advantage of a signal that was intentionally made public. The flip side is that if you're the one looking for a signal and you happen to find your neighbor's wireless LAN, the odds seem fairly slim that you'll be punished for it.

Estimates vary on the percentage of unprotected wireless LANs, but many observers agree on the main reason: It's too complicated for the average consumer to set up.

All certified Wi-Fi gear made since late 2003 are equipped with WPA (Wi-Fi Protected Access), an encryption system strong enough for business use, and earlier approved products have at least WEP (Wired Equivalent Privacy), a weaker system. Even WEP will force a would-be intruder to do some work, and most snoopers will just move on to the next unprotected LAN, Girard said.

However, consumers often don't use either because they aren't aware of the problem or can't figure out the startup process. For example, setting up WPA requires the new Wi-Fi user to come up with a good "pass phrase," type it into the computer, and then enter it on the router via the network, said David Cohen, senior product marketing manager at Wi-Fi chip maker Broadcom Corp.

Broadcom recently moved to simplify the process with Secure Easy Setup, a system that automatically creates a pass phrase and lets the user set up WPA just by clicking on a software button on the PC and then pushing a hardware button on the router. Secure Easy Setup is now shipping with products from Cisco Systems Inc.'s Linksys division, the biggest seller of home Wi-Fi gear, and will be adopted by other vendors that use Broadcom chips, Cohen said.

The Wi-Fi Alliance, the industry group that certifies Wi-Fi gear, wants to ensure easier setup for all consumers. In the first half of next year, it plans to create a standard that vendors can build in and have certified as a check-off item on their products, said Frank Hanzlik, the organization's managing director. The standard won't be required on all Wi-Fi products because it wouldn't be appropriate for complex enterprise gear installed by IT professionals, he added.

Some consumers will still choose to leave their networks open as a public service, the EFF's Bankston said. In addition to possibly violating the terms of your broadband contract, that move calls for all the safeguards mentioned above.

"If you don't know how to control network permissions, you should not run open Wi-Fi," Bankston said. "Even if you know what you're doing, opening up your network to the public will increase your risk."

8

The Unauthorized Use of Available Wireless Signals Should Not Be Illegal

John C. Dvorak

John C. Dvorak, a contributing editor to PC Magazine *since 1986, has won eight national awards from the Computer Press Association. His radio show, "Real Computing," can be heard on National Public Radio.*

With wi-fi technology becoming ubiquitous in urban areas, it is easy for an innocent user to connect to an unauthorized signal from a neighbor or nearby business. Unfortunately "poaching" someone else's wi-fi access is illegal in some places. This needs to change and the wi-fi signals bouncing around in many urban areas should be considered public domain, that is, there should be no legal restrictions on their use. Companies that want to limit access to their wi-fi need to use encryption technology. The burden of responsibility must be on the broadcaster, not on the casual user whose computer grabs the first wi-fi signal available in a certain area.

To drive around looking for connections to open wireless access points is called wardriving. In Canada, people who are caught doing this can be arrested for stealing bandwidth. The legality of this practice in the U.S., however, is a bit hazy, and there are many mitigating factors. One is that several organizations deliberately leave access points unencrypted so that people can use them as necessary. Also, many computers with built-in wireless simply grab the first signal they detect. Then there's the trespassing issue: The wardriver isn't trespassing on the router, the router is trespassing on the wardriver's airspace.

Free Access

This issue was brought home to me recently when one of my laptops told me it was ready to install new Windows XP upgrades, even though the laptop was not on a network and my wireless access point was off-line. I discovered that a neighbor's wireless router, named "default," had provided the access. Using my Toshiba's View Wireless Connections option, I saw five nearby networks that I could grab, three of which were unencrypted. Obviously there's plenty of free access around for harried travelers. It seems to me that being able to download your e-mail at an open connection is a good thing.

Look into the legality of this, though, and you hear vague comments like "The FBI doesn't know how legal it is" or "It may be illegal, because you're using someone else's connection or you're spying on their network." This issue will create ridiculous legal problems, which is bad news for both consumers and law enforcement, unless a sensible, national policy can be developed.

Personal and Corporate Responsibility

Let me jump in and propose a simple, logical public policy. Law enforcement doesn't need to get involved whenever some guy in a doughnut shop poaches a nearby Wi-Fi connection to check his e-mail, thinking he's on the shop's network. This shouldn't be a crime, even if he's intentionally poaching. We must put the burden of responsibility on the broadcaster, not the end user. It has to be made clear that people sending open connections all over town should be responsible for them.

Here's what I propose: Once a wireless signal leaves private property, it becomes public domain. If the person transmitting the signal wants it protected, then encryption is up to him or her. If someone beams an Internet connection into my home and I happen to lock onto the signal, he is trespassing on me, not the other way around. Public policy must reflect this logic. Keep it out of my house if you don't want me using it. Keep it out of my car. Keep it away from me in public places.

My computer grabs wireless signals impinging on my house more often than it grabs my own ... connection.

The Public Interest

This policy makes sense because it lets anyone who wants to provide open access to do so without hassle or fear. Groups in San Francisco and Seattle are openly promoting free 802.11 [wireless] connectivity. Many coffee shops, restaurants, and community groups now provide free wireless access, and directories of these hot spots are easy to find online.

This ubiquity of access is to be encouraged as in the public interest. But it can't happen if the law doesn't make the person transmitting the 802.11 signal responsible, instead of blaming any roaming users who are simply grabbing open connections. If this means that a corporate network is wide open to hackers, because the company doesn't bother encrypting the signal it broadcasts all over town, then so be it.

We must not follow the Canadian model that views using unprotected 802.11 connections as bandwidth theft. My computer grabs wireless signals impinging on my house more often than it grabs my own 802.11 connection. It just does. Agencies shouldn't be required to sort this out; it would be a law enforcement nightmare. In fact, it's in the public interest to discourage law enforcement intervention in this area, or I could be arrested for accidentally connecting to another person's router, when I didn't want to connect to it in the first place. That's ridiculous. I'm sure that no cops want to get involved in this mess either.

If you feel as strongly about this as I do, send this column to your Congressperson and tell him or her what you think. Together, we can make a difference if we speak up early.

9

Wireless Implants Enable the Government to Track and Control Citizens

Amy Worthington

Amy Worthington is an independent researcher and writer whose articles on the harmful effects of radio frequency identification, cell phones, and depleted uranium munitions appear in the Idaho Observer.

Government agencies have plans to use wireless technology as a means of tracking and controlling American citizens. Under the guise of a national ID system meant to improve national security, credit cards, driver's licenses, state-issued ID cards, and birth certificates will soon contain radio frequency identification (RFID) technology. With sensors located in utility poles and public buildings, this will allow the government to track the movements of every citizen. This will allow the government to store an individual's financial transactions, medical data, school records, and even religious and political affiliations in a centralized computer database available to authorities using handheld computers. The ultimate use of wi-fi technology comes in the form of RFID devices implanted under the skin that will allow the government to track individuals from birth to death. Americans must resist any attempt by despotic officials to use tracking devices to control its citizens. If they submit, the United States will become a police state where the "big brother" of authoritarian government will control the actions of every person.

The grand finale of American fascism is yet to come. No totalitarian ruling structure would be complete without an oppressive identification system that allows the dictator's henchmen to access birth-to-death information on every citizen listed in the national database. It's becoming obvious that no one is intended to escape the dictator's dynamic plans to force upon us national ID cards and, eventually, under-the-skin identification implants and a satellite tracking system able to keep each of us under round-the-clock surveillance.

The CIA [Central Intelligence Agency] admits that for years it has supported the rise of numerous U.S. technology companies for the development of hardware and software useful for surveillance and tracking of the masses. Oracle Corporation, the world's largest database software maker, is one of these CIA receptacles. As a voice for spooks everywhere, Oracle's billionaire chairman Larry Ellison has long demanded that Americans be encumbered with digital identification cards, complete with biometric markers such as hand prints and iris scans. Immediately after 9/11, Ellison presented to federal officials his proposal to create a national ID system with Oracle's expertise and technology. This system will provide ruling fascists with utmost efficiency at sucking detailed personal information on every citizen into what Ellison calls a "single comprehensive national security file."

The U.S. Intelligence Reform Bill of 2004 made a portion of Ellison's proposal into law. It requires that each new U.S. citizen born be issued a Social Security number to be included on his birth certificate along with his DNA biomarkers. All of this information will be stored in the national data base and no child will enroll in public school or receive any entitlement benefit without first presenting his Homeland Security birth certificate.

A National ID System

The Real ID Act passed by Congress in December 2005 completely solidified Ellison's ID plan. This new law establishes a massive, centrally-coordinated federal ID database. It forces all 50 states to spend millions of dollars to update their equipment so that by 2008, all holders of U.S. drivers licenses and state licensed ID cards will have their biometric data and other personal information fed directly into the national data base. [Texas] Congressman [Ron] Paul says the new ID cards will likely contain radio frequency identification tracking technology that can be read by scanners at a distance, allowing the governments of U.S., Canada and Mexico to quickly locate any card-bearing American.

We are told that banks and credit card companies applaud a national ID system. Instead of using bank credit and debit cards, people may eventually make purchases by showing their biometric Homeland ID cards. These financial transactions will then end up in the federal database, permitting fascists to assess our motives and intentions by monitoring our cashless sales and purchases.

One day soon, officials at all levels will be able to feed a citizen ID number into a wireless handheld or laptop device that connects to the national database. They may then instantly access that person's financial transactions, credit reports, medical and vaccination records, school records, driving records, political and religious affiliations and anything else that might have been inserted into his file by Homeland spies. ... And conversely, while Americans are being set up to surrender every shard of personal privacy, their fascist government is withholding from them more information than ever and continually expanding ways of shrouding data, according to a coalition of watchdog groups.

A Global Identity System

National ID cards are only the beginning. America's fascist police state is demonstrably anxious to ensure that each citizen have his identification number permanently attached to his body. For many years, U.S. intelligence agencies have been working with private corporations and covens of scientists from Princeton University and other enclaves to develop sub-dermal radio frequency devices that can be injected under the skin of humans for identification purposes. Syringe implantable ID transponders were readied years ago, as illustrated by the prototype fully developed in 1995 by CIA-connected Hughes Aircraft Company.

The corporate gargoyle chosen by the fascists to market ID implant devices for our new security state is Applied Digital Solutions (ADS). With corporate offices in Florida, ADS and its web of subsidiaries are now unleashing upon the world a vast variety of injectable ID chips, plus the sensors and scanners needed to read them.

A leading ADS backer is IBM, which promotes a global identity system. It's a matter of public record that IBM's New York office provided the German Nazis with technology and equipment that allowed Hitler to number and track concentration camp prisoners as well as others caught in his fascist web. If he could see his old partners now, Adol[f] might be green with envy, having been consigned to the barbaric practice of simply tattooing ID numbers on his slaves.

People in Europe are now being implanted with VeriPay chips in order to enter bars and nightclubs.

While many European nations are also setting up electronic identity systems as a foundation for future ID chip implants, it is especially pertinent that ADS has been given a prestigious award for its sinister implant technology by the World Economic Forum (WEF). WEF is a clique of wealthy corporate and political elitists who dictate global agendas. One of its most famous members is Bill Gates of Microsoft. Gates travels the world spending millions to promote injections for people of Third World nations. ID microchip implants are the MOTHER of all injections. Microsoft recently patented a way to use human skin as a power conduit for electronic devices.

In 2004, Tommy Thompson, at that time the Secretary of Health and Human Services under Homeland Security, invited ADS to a government showcase to promote the implantation of subdermal microchips as part of the U.S. health care system. Requiring no medical control studies on the health effects of microchip implantation, the FDA [Food and Drug Administration], which also gave us silicone breast implants, [the sugar substitute] aspartame and [the anti-inflammatory drug] Vioxx, has approved the marketing of certain ADS chips.

Tommy Thompson has now joined the ADS board. He told Americans during an interview with CBS Market Watch that ID chips inserted into our bodies will be a giant step towards achieving an electronic medical record for all Americans. While ADS is donating to medical facilities expensive scanners required to read its subdermal chips, the Department of Health and Human Services is providing grants to medical providers who will help build electronic health records for Americans within a decade.

These devices will ultimately offer "a new form of human slavery based on location control. They pose the greatest threat to personal freedom ever faced in human history."

Accepting Chip Implants

ADS and its subsidiaries, including VeriChip Corporation, have developed several kinds of implantable subdermal chips. One type is the FDA-approved VeriChip, that spits out the implantee's ID number when it is scanned by a chip reader. Another is the VeriPay device which carries financial information and is scanned like a debit card. People in Europe are now being implanted with VeriPay chips in order to enter bars and nightclubs.

So far, these kinds of chips are passive. That is, they don't beam information continuously. Their transponders have to be awakened by a reader. These chips and their scanners pass kilohertz radio-frequency signals back and forth through the skin. The first step to inducing public acceptance of these ID chips, said San Francisco Gate columnist Mark Morford, is getting the public to accept chip implants as beneficial for health. The next step is to make it fun and commercial and convenient. The third step is "whatever the hell they want."

VeriChip Corporation recently announced that already 68 U.S. medical facilities, including 65 hospitals, have now agreed to implement its VariMed system for patient and staff identification and tracking. This includes both implantable and wearable ID chips that will tie the health records of patients into Big Brother's electronic national database. In New Jersey, Hackensack University Medical Center and Trinitas Hospital will be implanting patients in their emergency rooms. These crafty hucksters are targeting the most vulnerable people first—the injured and the sick who are desperate for care, plus the homeless and mentally retarded who can't defend themselves.

As injectable ID chips come on line, Homeland Security is paying numerous corporations to develop a national network of object-mounted wireless sensors that will be able to read implanted human chips. This network of sensors will eventually relay information on the whereabouts and activities of implantees to teams of surveillance specialists. Conceivably, every wall socket could become a reader for implanted chips. To quote University of Kansas professor Jerry Dobson, these devices will ultimately offer "a new form of human slavery based on location control. They pose the greatest threat to personal freedom ever faced in human history."

A Tracking Chip

The argument that implanted chips will protect people from identity theft recently evaporated when researcher Jonathan

Westhues demonstrated on the Internet how easy it is to decode a VeriChip number implanted in a person's arm and then program another chip with that same number. Passive ID subdermal chips are the "good news" compared to grotesque ACTIVE implant chips also developed by ADS. The implantable Digital Angel is a grotesque communication device that can continually relay information wirelessly to either ground stations or to satellite systems. Developed to be a true tracking chip like the bulky radio ankle bracelets locked onto prisoners, it is tiny enough to be implanted into human flesh. The Angel has a built-in GPS [Global Positioning System] receiver and a wireless transceiver. In December, 2004, ADS signed an agreement with the satellite telecommunications company ORBCOMM. Such collusion will one day turn implanted citizens into walking radio beacons, trackable by satellite. Digital Angel is the ultimate in totalitarian control, to date Big Fascist Brother's most "cool tool."

The human body is not compatible with microwave radiation and bodies subjected to it 24-7 will ultimately be destroyed.

ADS has also developed a new Bio-Therm chip implant which can read and transmit to monitoring devices a person's temperature. In the works are other chips for identifying blood pressure, disease and hormonal levels. Reportedly, these biochips will be capable of relaying information to both satellite and ground stations. Oracle is backing a powerful new 999 medical biochip that contains a Pentium microprocessor just 2 mm square. This computerized sensor is being implanted into diabetics by doctors experimenting in London. Text messages from the chip's sensors will travel through flesh to a cell phone tethered to the patient, then on to monitoring stations.

In 2000, ADS chairman Richard Sullivan said that Digital Angel "relates directly to the exploding wireless marketplace."

He added, "We'll be demonstrating for the first time ever that wireless telecommunications systems and bio-sensor devices—capable of measuring and transmitting critical body function data—can be successfully linked together with GPS technology and integrated with the internet." Most sinister is the fact that these chips can be "activated" by distant monitoring facilities and they can be "written to" wirelessly, allowing the fascists to furtively add information that the chip bearer may know nothing about.

Bombarded with Radiation

Powerful web-enabled tracking chips which send and receive information at long distances are ultra radiation-intensive. Satellites communicate in microwave frequencies. Big Brother's most cool tool will be "hotter" than the hinges of Hell. Bodies bearing these chips will be continuously bombarded with incoming and outgoing microwave radiation, most likely in the megahertz or gigahertz range, the same frequencies employed by cell phones. Last October, *Time* magazine gave a plug to implantable ID and bio chips, stating they could save lives. But people who have active chips imbedded in their bodies will be dead men walking. The human body is not compatible with microwave radiation and bodies subjected to it 24-7 will ultimately be destroyed.

The fascists know this but, as Sullivan explained, the mighty global surveillance system now under construction is absolutely dependent upon wireless microwave transmissions. This is precisely why Americans have never been told the terrible truth about what the hand held wireless devices they cuddle to their bodies are already doing to their health, to their fragile memory centers and to their withering immune systems. In the Homeland Security state, microchip implants of various kinds will likely become as common as cell phones. Eventually, citizens who refuse to accept identification chips may be denied access to services and benefits by heel-clickers supervising the national ID system.

Make the choice to keep microwave-driven wireless devices as far away from your body as you can get them.

And thus we see how cleverly Americans are being manipulated into this crucible by killers in the White House, and by the most corrupt Congress in history and by the amoral, money-grubbing corporate megalith they all rode in on. In the name of national security and public health, millions of non-discerning citizens will allow themselves to be microchipped like dogs, tracked by satellite and stripped of all privacy as they become the virtual slaves of a techno-tyrannical surveillance state.

The Most Advanced Police State

If we want to know what USA will be like in the near future, we need only look at Tony Blair's Great Britain—surely the most advanced police state in Europe:

- ID cards with facial scans will soon be compulsory throughout the U.K.

- There are over 4 million closed circuit cameras monitoring every move the British people make and all faces caught on camera can be matched with a national data bank.

- British police are carrying hand held DNA kits linked to national data bases for when they test saliva.

- People are being pulled off London trains at random and forced to submit to a full body backscatter X-ray to reveal what they have under their clothes.

- Swipe cards used for transportation and building entry allow police to plot a citizen's every move on a dot map.

- All moving vehicles in Britain are camera-recorded so that police can analyze, by license number, every journey, and every gas purchase made.

- People and vehicles are being tracked from cell towers with a new technology called "Celldar" (as in radar).

- The British people are reporting grave illnesses from their exposure to thousands of microwave transmitters which make this metastasizing surveillance nightmare possible.

Microwave Transmitters Are Weapons

In part two of this discussion, we will document the latest scientific information on the devastating health effects that will result from the implanted microwave devices used to track and control slaves of the state. If you feel a creeping allergy to the fascism we have documented here, you can do something about it now. Make the choice to keep microwave-driven wireless devices as far away from your body as you can get them. These devices include all wireless telephones—both cell and household cordless—plus wireless computers, headphones and all other gadgets empowered by megahertz or gigahertz frequencies. If you must use wireless phones for business or emergencies, use speaker phones only. Never put a wireless device on your body, least of all near your precious brain. You are going to NEED a brain to survive—and ultimately defeat—fascist America.

Microwave transmitters are not toys; they are weapons. Brother's wireless revolution has induced millions of fools to voluntarily point these weapons at their own heads. The wireless revolution is not only about money, it is about control. It is about acclimatizing the masses to accept the dehumanizing parameters of Orwellian surveillance. A police state best flourishes when its citizens are sick, dimwitted cyborgs who are easy to track and control.

The "cool tool" communications microchip can also be used by the fascists to impose behavior modification. The CIA has decades of experience in using various microwave frequencies to misalign and confound the human brain in order to trigger prescribed behavior patterns. As the police state broadens with the help of Homeland Security's cooperating telcom players, it is conceivable that such devilish frequencies could be used with evil intent against all those who are "connected." These hapless victims, driven to and fro by fascist propaganda, will be oblivious to what is channeled into their sizzling brain neurons, into their internal organs, into their very souls by the deadly wireless transceivers they bear in their flesh.

Peter Zhou, chief scientist for the development of Digital Angel, declared that the subdermal identification/communication implants will make humans "a hybrid of electronic intelligence and our own soul." He is right! America's parasitic police state and all of its perversions absolutely ARE a soul thing. So the time has surely come to stand back and scrutinize this illicit monstrosity which so brazenly deceives, swindles, sickens and murders the people to gain power and wealth. Please start thinking about how you and your family are going to exist for a time in a demon-driven world where deadly radio frequency identification implants become mandatory.

The more people who courageously resolve to stand firm against this mighty beast, the safer we will be until we get through what is hopefully the final fascist interlude in human history.

10

Fears of Wireless Implant Surveillance Are Overblown

Josh McHugh

Josh McHugh is a contributing editor at Wired.

Radio frequency identification (RFID) devices have the ability to save lives and stop certain types of crime. The tiny RFID chips, which may be implanted under the skin, can be programmed to contain important medical information that doctors can print out when an unconscious patient is wheeled into an emergency room. In addition, chips may soon be used to prevent crimes or track criminals on parole. Since the chips can only be read at a distance of about thirty feet, there is little fear that the government will be able to follow innocent citizens from afar. Although conspiracy theorists fear that RFID chips will turn the United States into an authoritarian state, they have little to fear from these useful devices.

[In October 2004] the FDA [Food and Drug Administration] approved an implantable, rice-grain-sized microchip for use in humans. The tiny subcutaneous RFID [radio frequency identification] chip, made by a company called VeriChip, is being marketed as a lifesaving device. If you're brought to an emergency room unconscious, a scanner in the hospital doorway will read your chip's unique ID. That will unlock your medical records from a database, allowing doctors to learn about your penicillin allergy or your pacemaker.

That all sounds great, but could chip implants be used for something more sinister? Scott Silverman, the CEO of VeriChip's parent corporation, acknowledges that RFID injections aren't an easy sell. In fact, the company's own research reveals that 9 out of 10 people find the whole thing creepy.

Nothing makes privacy lovers and conspiracy theorists blanch like people rolling up their sleeves to get injected with tiny electronic devices. But fears of an Enemy of the State–like government tracking system overlook the fact that RFID chips can only be read at very short range. Will the chips let the FBI and National Security Agency watch implantees on some super-secret radar screen? Not likely. Could some stalker hobbyist hide a dozen RFID scanners around your neighborhood and track you from his garage? Possibly.

Thwarting Crime

VeriChip's biggest human-chip market is Mexico. Eighteen members of the attorney general's staff were implanted with a chip in order to control access to a new government facility. Building security isn't the biggest part of VeriChip's south-of-the-border sales pitch, though. Mexico's kidnapping wave— the country's 3,000 abductions a year are second only to Colombia worldwide—has led VeriChip to partner with the National Foundation for the Investigation of Lost and Kidnapped Children. So far, 1,000 Mexican citizens have voluntarily had RFID chips implanted.

The idea of using RFID gear to thwart kidnappers betrays a fundamental misunderstanding—or a deliberate misrepresentation—of how the technology works. An RFID implant is useful for tracking within a controlled area like a warehouse— "Where's widget No. 4,343?"—but not so useful for the kind Tommy Lee Jones does in *The Fugitive*. The RFID readers now on the market have a maximum range of about 30 feet. To monitor kidnappings in progress, Mexico would need to install RFID readers in every building, office, store, and street corner.

Silverman concedes that the company's Mexican distributor may not have tried very hard to dispel the notion that VeriChips have GPS [Global Positioning System] capabilities, which would be required for real remote tracking. VeriChip's parent company says a subdermal GPS device is now in development. But until a GPS implant becomes reality, implanted RFID chips will come in handy mostly in identifying dead bodies—that is, assuming kidnappers have the decency not to dig the chips out of their victims' arms. There are implementation problems with that fantasy RFID medical scheme, too. Once you've been chipped, you'll have to wait for VeriChip to connect its database—containing your medical records—with each hospital's individual system. By the time we get a national medical database, you'll probably have died of natural causes.

The Positive Side

Maybe you shouldn't trust RFID to stop a kidnapping or to save your life in an emergency. Perhaps a more realistic suggestion is to use RFID implants to replace the tracking bracelets now imposed upon those who a) aren't trusted to be in the right place at the right time; and b) aren't given much of a choice: kids (at theme parks like Fort Lauderdale's Wannado City and Legoland in Denmark), the elderly, and prisoners. Though injection is unpleasant to think about, subdermal devices are far harder to remove—and, thus, far more reliable—than an external bracelet. And what about the lighter side of chip injection? Patrons of Barcelona's Baja Beach Club now pay for drinks via a system that links their VeriChip implants to their credit cards.

Any potential revolution in human tracking or mundane convenience comes with a fundamental insecurity. A scanner operating at the right wavelength can read an RFID chip. That means that any hobbyist can just buy an RFID reader and use it to keep tabs on the chip-implanted people that happen to walk by. . . . It wouldn't be hard for a tech-savvy stalker to rig his scanner to activate a camera whenever it detected an RFID chip. By logging the times that your implant was scanned, he could easily track your comings and goings.

You could make your RFID chip unreadable by putting a blocking device like Mylar fabric or a metal plate between the chip and the reader. RFID chips could also be made to transmit their information in encrypted form, but VeriChip hasn't announced any plans to do so. Until it does, it might be best to keep RFID chips outside your epidermis. And a special message for all you kids out there: If your parents insist on microchip implantation, just make sure you've got some Mylar armbands lying around the house.

11

Cell Phones Transmit Dangerous Radiation That Causes Cancer

Taraka Serrano

Taraka Serrano is a health advocate associated with BIOPRO Technology, a company that provides protective tools for people who use cellular telephones.

Cell phones are tiny microwave transmitters that can cause a multitude of health problems. Studies conducted by several respected research institutions have concluded that microwave radiation is extremely dangerous and can be traced to several types of cancer. Children are particularly susceptible to this form of radiation. The telecom industry is aware of the fact that the cell phones are bombarding people with dangerous levels of microwave radiation but have failed to issue warnings. With millions of people using cell phones every day, cancer rates are increasing at an alarming level. Users of these dangerous phones should limit their exposure and demand that that industry devise ways to protect Americans from this insidious hazard.

In 1993, a man filed a lawsuit against the cell phone industry, claiming that his wife died from a brain tumor caused by her repeated use of the cell phone. The tumor was on the same side of the head where she held her cell phone and was shaped like the cell phone antenna. The case got widespread media attention and was featured in CNN's Larry King show.

Although the claim was dismissed by the court due to lack of sufficient evidence, it was a public relations nightmare for the wireless industry. It also marked the beginning of the global search for a definitive answer to the question: are cell phones safe or not? Does it cause cancer and other degenerative diseases? Brain cancer is up 25% since cell phones became popular. Every year, there are 183,000 more cases in the U.S. alone. Some health experts say there's a link with cell phone use, but is there proof?

The first evidence of a cancer link that shook the cell phone industry came in 1997.

In an effort to diffuse the negative publicity from the high-profile lawsuit, the cell phone industry itself funded a $25 million research program to prove that cell phones are safe. After 6 years of intensive research, however, the results were not what they were looking for. Dr. George Carlo, the chief research scientist of the program, found evidence that cell phones pose some health risks, possibly even cancer.

The first evidence of a cancer link that shook the cell phone industry came in 1997. Dr. Michael Repacholi and his colleagues from the Royal Adelaide Hospital in South Australia reported that long-term exposure to the type of radiation that comes from digital cell phones caused an increase in the occurrence of lymphoma in mice. The study received widespread international media attention because it was the first time that cancer has been linked to the cell phone in a well-conducted study.

The Red Flags: Solving the Cancer Puzzle

In order to show a link between cell phone radiation and cancer, let's look at several studies Dr. Carlo investigated that made him blow the whistle, so to speak. These red-flag findings provide the pieces that fit together to form the cancer picture:

- DNA Damage in Human Blood Studies

- Breakdown in the Blood-Brain Barrier

- Studies of Tumors in People Who Use Cell Phones

- Studies of Cell Phone Radiation Dosage and Response

DNA Damage in Human Blood

All tumors and all cancers are the result of genetic damage. Most often that damage includes the formation of micronuclei—fragments of chromosomes that form membranes around themselves and appear under a microscope as additional nuclei in blood cells (which normally have just a single nucleus). The relationship between micronuclei and cancer is so strong that doctors around the world test for their presence to identify patients likely to develop cancer. The presence of micronuclei indicates that the cells can no longer properly repair broken DNA. This deficiency is considered to be an indication of an increased risk of developing cancer.

In December 1998, Drs. Ray Tice and Graham Hook of Integrated Laboratory Systems in North Carolina have shown that blood cells exposed to cell phone radiation suffer genetic damage in the form of micronuclei. In their studies, DNA and chromosome damage in human white blood cells occurred when exposed to signals from all types of phones—analog, digital, and PCS. Damage was shown even from signals occurring at a SAR level below the government's "safety" guideline.

Using different methods, the above finding was confirmed by Dr. Joseph Roti Roti of Washington University in St. Louis in 2000. His research showed that human blood cells exposed to radiation at wireless phone frequencies did indeed develop genetic damage, in the form of micronuclei. This finding received a lot of notice because Dr. Roti Roti is a prominent scientist who does his work under funding by Motorola Inc.

This has a very serious implication. If cell phone radiation encourages the formation of micronuclei in blood cells, and micronuclei are said to be "biological markers" for cancer, then based on these studies alone cell phone use could be said to increase the risk of cancer.

Breakdown in the Blood-Brain Barrier

The blood-brain barrier is a special filter in the blood vessels of the brain that keeps dangerous chemicals from reaching sensitive brain tissue and causing DNA breaks and other damage.

In 1994 and again, in 2002, Dr. Leif Salford from Lund University in Stockholm, Sweden found in his studies that rats exposed to cell phone radiation showed a breakdown in the blood-brain barrier, as well as areas of shrunken, damaged neurons.

The micronuclei studies of Tice, Hook and Roti Roti and the blood-brain findings of Salford provide a two-step explanation for how cancer could be caused by cell phone radiation.

Step One: A leakage or breakdown in the blood-brain barrier would provide a pathway for cancer-causing chemicals in the bloodstream (from tobacco, pesticides, air pollution, etc.) to leak into the brain and damage sensitive brain tissue that would otherwise be protected. These chemicals could break the DNA in the brain or cause other harm to reach those cells.

Step Two: While a number of studies showed that cell phone radiation by itself does not appear to break DNA, the micronuclei findings suggest that they do impair the DNA repair mechanisms in brain cells. Micronuclei result from a breakdown of the cell's ability to repair itself. If the brain cells become unable to repair themselves, then carcinogenesis—the creation of tumors—induced by chemical toxins could begin.

DNA carries the genetic material of an organism and its different cells. Any damage that goes unrepaired affects the future generation of cells. The change has procreated and this mutation is seen as a possible cause of cancer.

Users of handheld cell phones have more than twice the risk of dying from brain cancer than do car phone users—whose antennas are mounted on the body of the car.

Tumors in People Who Use Cell Phones

Epidemiological studies, performed by different investigators using different methods, show some evidence of an increased risk of tumors among people who use cellular phones.

In 1998, Dr. Ken Rothman of Epidemiology Resources, Inc. in Newton, Mass., did a study showing that users of handheld cell phones have more than twice the risk of dying from brain cancer than do car phone users—whose antennas are mounted on the body of the car, far removed from the users' heads.

In 1998, Joshua Muscat, a research scientist from the American Health Foundation, showed in his study a doubling of the risk of developing neuro-epithelial tumors on the outside of the brain among cell phone users, particularly on the side of the skull where cell phone antennas are held during calls.

Muscat also showed in another study that people who have used cell phones for six years or more have a 50-percent increase in risk of developing acoustic neuroma, a benign tumor of the nerve that controls hearing and extends from the ear to the brain. Acoustic neuromas can cause hearing loss and can be life-threatening if untreated.

This was confirmed in a separate study in Stockholm, Sweden by Anders Ahlbom in 2004 and sponsored by the World Health Organization (WHO), which finds that people who have used cell phones, this time for at least 10 years, may have an increased risk of developing acoustic neuroma.

In a study also requested by WHO [World Health Organization], researchers headed by Dr. Lennart Hardell of the Orebro Medical Center in Sweden examined 1,617 patients aged between 20 and 80 who had been diagnosed with a brain tumor between 1997 and 2000. They were then compared to healthy people. Those who used cell phones for less than 10 years faced a 20% higher risk of developing brain cancer. But for those who used them for more than a decade the risk was 80% higher. The study also found that tumors were 2.5 times more likely to be on the same side of the head as the phone was held. The cancer of the auditory nerve, accoustic neuroma, showed a larger increase—3.5 times greater risk.

The big picture is disturbingly clear. There is a definite risk that the radiation plume that emanates from a cell phone antenna can cause cancer and other health problems.

Cell Phone Radiation Dosage and Response

All studies mentioned showed that an increase in cell phone radiation exposure also increases the likelihood of the adverse effect occurring.

In Repacholi's study of mice, the risk of lymphoma increased significantly the longer the mice were exposed to the radio waves.

In the research work done by Tice, Hook, and Roti Roti, the risks of genetic damage as measured by micronuclei formation increased as the amount of radiation increased.

In the three epidemiological studies—two by Muscat and one by Hardell—the risk of tumors was greater in the areas of the brain near where the cell phone was held.

In Salford's study, the higher the radiation exposure level the rats were exposed to, the more damage was apparent in the blood vessels in the brain and the neurons.

The Big Cancer Picture

The test tube studies by Tice and Hook; the mouse study by Repacholi and Salford; and the epidemiological studies by Rothman, Muscat, and Hardell all agree in that they suggest an increased risk of cancer among cell phone users. They fit together to form the beginnings of a picture that everyone can see. They perhaps don't form the complete picture yet, but there are enough already in place to see that there is cause for genuine public health concern about cell phone safety.

According to Dr. Carlo, "The big picture is disturbingly clear. There is a definite risk that the radiation plume that emanates from a cell phone antenna can cause cancer and other health problems. It is a risk that affects hundreds of millions of people around the world. It is a risk that must be seen and understood by all who use cell phones so they can take all the appropriate and available steps to protect themselves—and especially to protect young children whose skulls are still growing and who are the most vulnerable to the risks of radiation."

More Pieces Coming

In 2000, a team of Sydney researchers published a scientific hypothesis about how mobile phone radiation causes cancer. The report claims that the radiation generated by cell phones causes ongoing stress to the body cells, causing them to give off "heat shock proteins (HSP)." The human cells sometimes release these proteins in response to injury or infection. Such a chronic activation of the heat shock response affects the normal regulation of cells, which could result in cancer.

In 2002, cell biologist Fiorenzo Marinelli and his team at the National Research Council in Bologna, Italy, exposed leukemia cells to continuous radio waves similar to that of cell phones. The exposed cells had a higher rate of death than the controls initially, but after further exposure, a curious thing happened: instead of more cells dying, the exposed cells were replicating furiously compared to the controls. Genes that trigger cells to multiply were turned on in a high proportion of the cells. The cancer, although briefly beaten back, had become more aggressive. Marinelli suspects that the radiation may initially damage DNA, and that this interferes with the biochemical signals in a way that ultimately triggers the cells to multiply more rapidly.

Darius Leszczynski at the Radiation and Nuclear Safety Authority in Helsinki found that one-hour exposure to mobile phone radiation caused cultured human cells to shrink. Leszczynski believes this happens when a cell is damaged. In a human being, such changes could destroy the blood-brain barrier. Radiation-induced changes in the cells could also interfere with normal cell death when the cell is damaged. If cells that are 'marked' to die do not, tumors can form.

So Why Are Cell Phones Still Around?

Now with all the mounting evidence, the cell phone industry still maintains their position that cell phones are safe and have even begun marketing towards children. The governments have been rather slow in stepping in to warn people of any danger from using cell phones. Fortunately, health officials and experts in several European countries are taking the first steps, having issued public warnings to parents urging caution about kids and cell phones.

If the previous environmental issues involving tobacco, asbestos, and lead are any indication, it takes years and even decades to accumulate the amount of evidence that would produce a definite ruling. In the case of cigarette smoking, it took two decades of study and 100 years of consumer use to gather enough data to meet research standards to demonstrate the need for the U.S. Surgeon General's warning label on cigarette packs. Some experts say that in the case of cell phones, it will not take that long as data are coming in at a faster pace. But at the present the authorities can only urge people to exercise caution.

Replication of research is another problem. A study that comes out with a new finding generally does not gain immediate acceptance in the scientific community or the wireless industry unless another research lab has been able to replicate the work and the findings. The industry has cleverly perpetuated their stance by creating an illusion of responsible follow up by always calling for more research.

When Dr. Salford published his study in 2003 showing that rat brain neurons were dying from exposure to cell phone radiation, he warned there might be similar effects in humans that over time could lead to degenerative diseases of the brain. His study was written off by the industry as a "novel" finding that needed to be replicated.

But achieving the scientific standard of replication can be complicated. Salford says if studies aren't absolutely replicated, providing an apples-to-apples comparison, there's wiggle room to dispute follow-up findings. Research studies also require funding, and the wireless industry, after Dr. Carlo's revelations, have been reluctant to put money into more comprehensive research. As for governments, again many European governments are taking the responsible course by funding research, but the U.S. and Canada are lagging poorly.

In 1999, CNN's Larry King once again featured a man who brought a multimillion dollar lawsuit against cell phone manufacturers. This time the man, a Maryland neurologist, was himself diagnosed with brain cancer—again located on the side of the head where he held his cell phone. The suit was yet again dismissed, however, and the man died not long afterwards.

According to a WHO report, [100 million] people have died from tobacco use in the 20th century, and 10 times as many will die in the 21st century. No one is suggesting that cell phones could cause as much casualties, but do we really want to wait and find out?

Aiming for Responsible Technology

Unlike tobacco, the cell phone has become as indispensable [a] part of our lives as [the] television and computer. It has enabled us to make a gigantic leap in the way we communicate with one another and has been credited widely with saving people's lives in emergency situations. Cell phones are here to stay, and perhaps rightly so.

The question is not how to stop people from using this ubiquitous device but rather how to make it safer. The first step always is to admit there is a problem, hence the industry and the government have to acknowledge the health risks inherent with the present technology. This way we can all find the proper solutions that we may more enjoy the benefits of its use without sacrificing our health and wellbeing.

12

Cell Phones Do Not Cause Cancer

James Niccolai

James Niccolai is a reporter for the IDG News Service.

Researchers in the United Kingdom (UK) have shown that cell phone users are not at an increased risk of contracting cancer. This study is one of many that prove cell phones to be harmless when used over an extended period. While critics continue to worry about the link between cell phones and cancer, cell phone users face a much greater risk of being injured in a car accident, especially if they talk on their cell phones while driving.

Using a mobile phone for ten years does not significantly increase a person's risk of developing a tumor, according to a new study from the UK's Institute of Cancer Research.

The investigation was the largest one to date that has studied the relationship between mobile phones and acoustic neuromas, a type of tumor that occurs close to the ear, according to the study's authors.

"The results of our study suggest that there is no substantial risk in the first decade after starting use. Whether there are longer-term risks remains unknown, reflecting the fact that this is a relatively recent technology," Anthony Swerdlow, professor and lead investigator at the Institute of Cancer Research, said in a statement.

The study looked at 678 people with acoustic neuromas and 3,553 people without the illness. They were asked detailed

James Niccolai, "No Substantial Risk in First Decade of Use, Researcher Says," www. pcworld.com, August 31, 2005. Reproduced by permission.

questions about their mobile phone use, including the length and frequency of the calls they made, the type of phone they used, and other factors that might affect their risk of getting the disease.

The study found no relation between risk of acoustic neuroma and level of mobile phone use.

Tumor Appearances

Acoustic neuromas are of particular interest because they occur close to where mobile phones are held to the head. They are a type of benign tumor that grows in the nerve connecting the ear to the brain. Acoustic neuromas often cause hearing loss and impair balance, but they do not typically spread to other parts of the body.

The study's results corroborate the findings of other recent reports, but since it recommends longer-term studies, the UK investigation may not put to rest the debate over whether cell phone radiation harms health.

Still, the test marks "a great step forward" in understanding the relationship between tumors and mobile phones because it involved such a large number of participants, the researchers said.

"The evidence for the health effects of mobile phones and radio-frequency fields in general has been reviewed by several expert committees quite recently, and the results of this new study are compatible with their conclusions," Minouk Schoemaker, one of the report's authors, wrote in an e-mail response to questions.

The study was published online in the *British Journal of Cancer*. It was conducted in the United Kingdom, Denmark, Finland, Norway, and Sweden—countries where mobile phones were introduced relatively early.

A separate study from Denmark, published in the journal *Neurology*, looked at two other types of tumor: glioma and meningioma. That study involved about 1200 participants, including 427 who suffered from one of the two diseases; it, too, found no increased risk of tumor development from cell phone use. Like the UK report, it advised that longer-term research be undertaken.

A further report released in January by the UK's National Radiological Protection Board acknowledged the absence of any conclusive evidence linking mobile phones to tumors or cancer; nevertheless it recommended that children's mobile phone use be limited, suggesting that they might be more vulnerable to radio frequency radiation exposure because their nervous systems are still developing.

The greatest health risk established to date involves the increased risk of accidents due to using a cell phone while driving.

Children Not Studied

This week's UK study looked at people between the ages of 18 and 69, and did not address the risks to children, Schoemaker said.

The Institute of Cancer Research is also studying other types of tumors, including glioma and meningioma. Results from those tests are not yet ready for release, she said.

Asked for her personal opinion about whether mobile phones pose a health risk, she replied that the greatest health risk established to date involves the increased risk of accidents due to using a cell phone while driving.

13

Cell Phone Use
Impairs Drivers

Lee Siegel

Lee Siegel is a science writer who has worked for the Associated Press in Los Angeles and Seattle, the Salt Lake Tribune, *and, currently, the University of Utah Public Relations. He is the co-author, with Robert B. Smith, of* Windows into the Earth: The Geological Story of Yellowstone and Grand Teton National Parks *(Oxford University Press, 2000).*

Young people who talk on cell phones while driving face an increased risk of accidents. A 2005 study that tracked driving skills of eighteen- to twenty-five-year-olds on driving simulators showed that the reflexes of test subjects talking on telephones were as slow as those of senior citizens who were not using phones. With cell phone use, the number of accidents for young people doubled, braking time slowed, and it took longer for subjects to regain speeds after slowing. Although young people have faster reflexes than senior citizens, talking on a cell phone negates this advantage. Those who wish to drive better than an elderly driver with slow reflexes should hang up the phone and pay attention to the road.

If you have been stuck in traffic behind a motorist yakking on a cellular phone, a new University of Utah study will sound familiar [2005]: When young motorists talk on cell phones, they drive like elderly people, moving and reacting more slowly and increasing their risk of accidents.

"If you put a 20-year-old driver behind the wheel with a cell phone, their reaction times are the same as a 70-year-old driver who is not using a cell phone. It's like instantly aging a large number of drivers," says David Strayer, a University of Utah psychology professor and principal author of the study.

Frank Drews, an assistant professor of psychology and study co-author, adds: "If you want to act old really fast, then talk on a cell phone while driving."

The new study by Strayer and Drews was published in this winter's issue of *Human Factors*, the quarterly journal of the Human Factors and Ergonomics Society.

The study found that when 18- to 25-year-olds were placed in a driving simulator and talked on a cellular phone, they reacted to brake lights from a car in front of them as slowly as 65- to 74-year-olds who were not using a cell phone.

The elderly drivers, meanwhile, became even slower to react to brake lights when they spoke on a cell phone. But the good news for elderly drivers was that their driving skills did not become as bad as had been predicted by earlier research showing that older people performing multiple tasks suffer additional impairment due to aging.

Motorists who talk on cell phones are more impaired than drunken drivers with blood alcohol levels exceeding 0.08.

The study found that drivers who talked on cell phones—regardless of whether they were young or old—were 18 percent slower in hitting their brakes than drivers who didn't use cell phones. The drivers chatting on cell phones also had a 12 percent greater following distance—an effort to compensate for paying less attention to road conditions—and took 17 percent longer to regain the speed they lost when they braked.

In addition, "there was also a twofold increase in the number of [simulated] rear-end collisions when drivers were conversing on cell phones," the study says.

Driving to Distraction

Strayer and his colleagues are widely known for their 2001 study showing that hands-free cell phones are just as distracting as hand-held cell phones, and for a 2003 study showing that the reason is "inattention blindness," in which motorists can look directly at road conditions but not really see them because they are distracted by a cell phone conversation. The research has called into question legislative efforts by various states to ban motorists from using handheld but not hands-free cell phones.

The same researchers also gained publicity for another study, which was presented at a scientific meeting in 2003, showing that motorists who talk on cell phones are more impaired than drunken drivers with blood alcohol levels exceeding 0.08.

The new study included 20 older adults (ages 65 to 74, with average age 70) and 20 younger adults (ages 18 to 25, with average age 20). All of them had normal vision and a valid driver's license. Preliminary tests showed older people were slower to process information, as was expected.

Then the psychologists had the young and older study participants "drive" in a high-tech driving simulator. Participants in the simulator used dashboard instruments, steering wheel and brake and gas pedals from a Ford Crown Victoria sedan, surrounded by three screens showing freeway scenes and traffic, including a "pace car" that intermittently hit its brakes 32 times as it appeared to drive in front of study participants. If a participant failed to hit their own brakes, they eventually would rear-end the pace car.

Each participant drove four simulated 10-mile freeway trips lasting about 10 minutes each, talking on a cell phone with a research assistant during half the trips and driving without talking the other half. Only hands-free phones were used to eliminate any possible distraction from manipulating a hand-held cell phone.

Thirty times each second, the simulator measured the participants' driving speed, following distance and—if applicable—how long it took them to hit the brakes and how long it took them to regain speed. Those factors "have been shown to affect the likelihood and severity of rear-end collisions," Strayer and Drews wrote.

The Findings: Age and Cell Phone Use Impair Drivers

The study found that:

—Compared with young drivers, older drivers were slower to hit the brakes when needed, tended to hit the brakes twice, took longer to regain speed and had a greater following distance. This was true when young and old participants drove with or without cell phones.

—Compared with drivers who did not talk on cell phones, those who used a cell phone while driving were slower to hit the brakes, had a longer following distance and took longer to regain speed. This was true of both young and old drivers. "Once drivers on cell phones hit the brakes, it takes them longer to get back into the normal flow of traffic," Strayer says. "The net result is they are impeding the overall flow of traffic."

—When young drivers used cell phones, the reaction time in hitting the brakes slowed to match that of elderly drivers who did not talk on cell phones, namely, an average of 912 milliseconds, or a bit more than nine-tenths of a second. When not talking on cell phones, young motorists hit the brakes within an average of 780 milliseconds, or almost eight-tenths of a second. The difference may seem small, but represents a 17 percent slower reaction time. Strayer says other studies have shown that much of a decrease in reaction time increases both the likelihood and severity of accidents.

—When elderly drivers used cell phones, their reaction times got worse, but not as bad as had been expected. Previous research "suggested older people should have been really messed up if you put them on a cell phone because, not only are they slower overall due to age, but there's a difficulty dividing attention that should make using a cell phone much more difficult for them than for young people," Strayer said. Yet the study "suggests older adults do not suffer a significantly greater penalty for talking on a cell phone while driving than do their younger counterparts," Strayer and Drews wrote.

That may be because older adults have more experience driving and take fewer risks, and those in the study may have been healthier than other seniors, Strayer says.

Twice as many accidents happened to motorists on cell phones compared with motorists who were not talking.

Crashing While Talking

Federal statistics show that the most accident-prone drivers are the young and old, with fatal accident rates high during teenage years, then declining until age 30 and staying relatively level until age 60, when accident rates climb again as age increases.

Six participants in the new study rear-ended the pace car while driving the simulator. Four accidents (one older adult and three younger adults) happened while the participants talked on cell phones. Two did not (one older adult and one younger adult).

There were too few collisions for statistical analysis. But Strayer notes that twice as many accidents happened to motorists on cell phones compared with motorists who were not talking. And young drivers were in collisions twice as often as elderly drivers.

"Older drivers were slightly less likely to get into accidents than younger drivers," Strayer says. "Why? They tend to have a greater following distance. Their reactions are impaired, but they are driving so cautiously they were less likely to smash into somebody," although in real life, "older drivers are significantly more likely to be rear-ended" because of their slow speed.

When Strayer and Drews combined the new accident data with simulated driving accidents in their earlier studies, they counted 12 rear-end collisions among 121 study participants. Ten of the collisions happened when motorists were talking on cell phones.

That is statistically significant and provides "clear evidence that drivers using a cell phone were more likely to be involved in a collision than when these same drivers were not using a cell phone," the psychologists wrote.

14

The Wi-Fi Revolution Is Failing the Urban Poor

Roberto Lovato

Roberto Lovato is a 2003 George Washington Williams fellow and a writer with Pacific News Service.

The wireless media in the United States is controlled by huge corporations that are denying low-cost wi-fi to black, Latino, Arab, and other minority communities. By doing so, the companies are creating a racial digital divide. People in the media reform movement must work closely with those in minority neighborhoods who are on the other side of the digital color line. Access to wi-fi and other technology is a life and death issue in the struggle for equal rights and equal opportunity in the United States and low cost wireless should be available to all citizens whatever their economic status.

W.E.B. Du Bois wrote at a time of breathtaking social change, a time not unlike our own. The black social critic, activist and writer documented how African Americans fled the bitter roots of sharecropping in the Jim Crow South only to find themselves at the margins of the bustling industrial economy of cities in the North like Philadelphia.

The railroad ushered in dramatic change and Philadelphia, a mercantile and industrial powerhouse, had taken its place as the center of the U.S. railroad industry. In books written in the 1890s and early 20th century, Du Bois captured how railroad barons and white labor union leaders forced African Americans into densely populated brick row homes on sewage-filled streets on the wrong side of the railroad tracks, away from the commerce and economic development on the other, whiter side.

Like those turn of the century railroads, the Internet has connected the entire country and transformed many industries. Were he alive today, Du Bois might similarly conclude that the digital divide has a color line running through it.

As was the case with ownership of and access to railroads in the industrial era, control over and access to broadband connectivity is defining global, regional and individual success. In turn, it is shaping whether African Americans, Latinos and the poor will continue to live in economically strip-mined neighborhoods like Philadelphia's Kensington.

Claiming unfair competition, representatives of big business lobbied Pennsylvania legislators to outlaw free municipal Wi-Fi for . . . 75 percent of Philadelphia's poor.

A Big Threat to Telecoms

[In 2004] city leaders announced a program to provide universal access to Wi-Fi, wireless technology that provides individuals and organizations with Internet connectivity. The city's Chief Information Officer, Diana Neff, proposed a strategy to "create a digital infrastructure for open-air Internet access and to help citizens, businesses, schools, and community organizations make effective use of wireless technology to achieve their goals."

But free to low-cost Wi-Fi access represents a threat to big telecoms and cable providers that reap billions by charging for Internet access while tapping into the publicly-owned electronic radio spectrum that facilitates wireless communications.

Like the railroad barons of Du Bois' time, the CEOs and lobbyists of telecom and cable giants worked against the interest of Philadelphia's majority. Claiming unfair competition, representatives of big business lobbied Pennsylvania legislators to outlaw free municipal Wi-Fi for the 75 percent of Philadelphia's poor who Neff estimates have no access to the Internet. Media reform advocates and local officials defeated those efforts earlier [in 2005] in a victory that has become a benchmark for activists in other cities. [The telecoms succeeded in 2006 when a law was passed that prevented municipalities in Pennsylvania from offering wi-fi.]

The Unbearable Whiteness of Media

Like many in the media reform movement, Du Bois might see the strategic import of securing universal Wi-Fi access in the City of Brotherly Love. Yet, unlike the members of the mostly white media reform movement (and unlike most U.S. "progressives"), he would work and live in Kensington or other poor, unwired neighborhoods and would organize there—just as he did when he helped establish the NAACP. Living and organizing among the poor informed his passion to fight what he called "the evil which a privileged few may exercise over the majority."

That such a spirit—and practice—is lacking in the media reform and larger progressive community bodes ill for political work in the United States. The media reform movement must adopt not just Du Bois' passion for issues like race, but his methods as well.

For now, a monochromatic color spectrum (as in various shades of white) divides the movement from people like Saskia Fischer, an organizer with the United Church of Christ's Media Empowerment Project. Consider her the exception to what some call the "unbearable whiteness of media reform." Fischer has heeded Du Bois' call to attack the color line by engaging working people in what she and others prefer to call the "media justice movement." The term "includes people of color—and is more radical," says Fischer. Fischer, herself a young Indian and Dutch immigrant, works with black, Latino, Arab, immigrant and other communities by linking licensing of the public spectrum, computer and internet access and other media issues to local concerns like education and jobs.

As effective as the organizing of media reform groups like The Center for Digital Democracy, the Media Access Project and Free Press is, the groups are increasingly recognizing the need to cross the color line in a country where most major cities are, like Philadelphia, "majority minority" cities. Organizing in and with non-white, working class communities will add vitality and urgency—and a large base.

Failure to broaden the movement comes at a time when the right is reengineering itself to be more inclusive. "Media justice issues are life and death issues for our communities," says Fischer. Learning to navigate the digital divide's color line may be similarly fateful for the progressive movement itself.

Organizations to Contact

The editors have compiled the following list of organizations concerned with the issues debated in this book. The descriptions are derived from materials provided by the organizations. All have publications or information available for interested readers. The list was compiled on the date of publication of the present volume; the information provided here may change. Be aware that many organizations take several weeks or longer to respond to inquiries, so allow as much time as possible.

Cato Institute
1000 Massachusetts Avenue NW
Washington, DC   20001-5403
(202) 842-0200 • fax: (202) 842-3490
e-mail: jblock@cato.org
Web site: www.cato.org/index.html

The Cato Institute is a nonprofit libertarian public policy research foundation headquartered in Washington, D.C. The Cato Institute seeks to broaden the parameters of public policy debate to allow consideration of the traditional American principles of limited government, individual liberty, free markets, and peace. The institute researches issues in the media and provides commentary for magazine, newspaper, and news shows editorials.

Center for Digital Democracy
1718 Connecticut Ave. NW, Suite 200
Washington, DC   20009
(202) 986-2220
e-mail: jeff@democraticmedia.org
Web site: www.democraticmedia.org

The Center for Digital Democracy is committed to preserving the openness and diversity of the Internet in the broadband era, and to realizing the full potential of digital communications through the development and encouragement of non-commercial, public interest programming. The group publishes press releases, reports on wi-fi communications and the telecom industry, articles, and op-ed pieces available through its Web site.

Consumers Union Wireless Watchdog

Consumers Union, Yonkers, NY   10703-1057
(914) 378-2455 • fax: (914) 378-2928
e-mail: www.consumersunion.org/wireless/feedback.html
Web site: www.consumersunion.org/wireless

Wireless Watchdog is run by Consumers Union, an independent, nonprofit testing and information organization serving only consumers. Through the Wireless Watchdog organization, users of wireless services can educate themselves concerning cell phone and wi-fi issues, file complaints against cell phone providers, and petition politicians and the Federal Communications Commission. In addition to publishing *Consumer Reports*, the group makes various reports available on its Web site concerning the digital divide, protection of phone records, and legislation relevant to the wi-fi issue.

Electronic Frontier Foundation (EFF)

PO Box 170190, San Francisco, CA   94117
(415) 668-7171 • fax: (415) 668-7007
e-mail: eff@eff.org
Web site: www.eff.org

EFF is an organization that aims to promote a better understanding of telecommunications issues. It fosters awareness of civil liberties issues arising from advancements in computer-based communications media and supports litigation to preserve, protect, and extend First Amendment rights in computing, wireless, and other telecommunications technologies. EFF's publications include *Building the Open Road, Crime and Puzzlement*, the quarterly newsletter *Networks & Policy*, the bi-weekly electronic newsletter *EFFector Online*, and online bulletins and publications, including *First Amendment in Cyberspace*.

Electronic Privacy Information Center (EPIC)
1718 Connecticut Ave. NW, Suite 200
Washington, DC   20009
(202) 483-1140 • fax: (202) 483-1248
e-mail: info@epic.org
Web site: www.epic.org

EPIC is an organization that advocates the public's right to electronic privacy. It sponsors educational and research programs, compiles statistics, and conducts litigation. Its publications include the biweekly electronic newsletter *EPIC Alert* and online reports.

Media Empowerment Project
Saskia Fischer, Washington, DC   20002
(800) 778-9214 • fax: (202) 543-5994
e-mail: fischers@ucc.org
Web site: www.ucc.org/ocinc/mep

The Media Empowerment Project grew out of the United Church of Christ's historic commitment to civil rights in media advocacy. The project is grounded in the belief that struggles for social, racial, and gender justice must address questions of media ownership, accountability, and Internet access in order to truly be effective. The organization works with people of color, women, and youth to help them think about how media could best serve their needs and advance their struggles for social justice. The group publishes an online organizing manual, a resource for those interested in starting media empowerment projects in their communities.

MuniWireless
(978) 921-1112
e-mail: amy@muniwireless.com
Web site: http://muniwireless.com

MuniWireless is the portal for news and information about citywide wireless broadband projects around the world. The organization publishes *MuniWireless* magazine, online reports that include guides for cities, municipal projects, and articles about various municipal wi-fi legislation.

Privacy International Washington Office
1718 Connecticut Ave. NW, Suite 200
Washington, DC 20009
(202) 483-1217 • fax: (202) 483-1248
e-mail: privacyint@privacy.org
Web site: www.privacy.org

Privacy International is an independent, nongovernmental organization whose goal is to protect the privacy rights of citizens worldwide. On its Web site the organization provides archives of material on privacy, including international agreements, the report *Freedom of Information and Access to Government Records Around the World*, and *Private Parts Online*, an online newsletter that reports recent stories on international privacy and wireless communications issues.

Privacy Rights Clearinghouse (PRC)
3100 5th Ave., Suite B, San Diego, CA 92103
(619) 298-3396 • fax: (619) 298-5681
e-mail: jbeebe@privacyrights.org
Web site: www.privacyrights.org

The Privacy Rights Clearinghouse (PRC) is a nonprofit consumer organization with a two-part mission—to provide consumer information and advocate for consumer privacy in the wireless era. The PRC's goals are to raise consumer awareness of how technology affects personal privacy; empower consumers to take action to control their own personal information by providing practical tips on privacy protection; respond to specific privacy-related complaints from consumers; and report on consumer issues in policy papers, testimony, and speeches. PRC's Web site provides texts of all fact sheets, transcripts of PRC speeches and testimony, FAQs, and stories of consumer experiences.

Bibliography

Books

Robert D. Austin and Stephen P. Bradley, eds.
The Broadband Explosion: Leading Thinkers on the Promise of a Truly Interactive World. Boston: Harvard Business School Press, 2005.

Lee Barken
Wireless Hacking Projects for Wi-Fi Enthusiasts. Rockland, MA: Syngress, 2004.

Annmarie Chandler and Norie Neumark, eds.
At a Distance: Precursors to Art and Activism on the Internet. Cambridge, MA: MIT Press, 2005.

Robert W. Crandall
Competition and Chaos: U.S. Telecommunications Since the 1996 Telecom Act. Washington, DC: Brookings Institution, 2005.

Andy Dornan
The Essential Guide to Wireless Communications Applications: From Cellular Systems to Wi-Fi. Upper Saddle River, NJ: Prentice Hall PTR, 2002.

Jeff Duntemann
Jeff Duntemann's Wi-Fi Guide. Scottsdale, AZ: Paraglyph, 2004.

Rob Flickenger and Roger Weeks
Wireless Hacks. Beijing: O'Reilly, 2006.

Wei Meng Lee
Windows XP Unwired: A Guide for Home, Office, and the Road. Sebastopol, CA: O'Reilly, 2003.

William C. Lee   *Wireless and Cellular Telecommunications.* New York: McGraw-Hill, 2006.

Robert W. McChesney, Russell Newman, and Ben Scott, eds.   *The Future of Media: Resistance and Reform in the 21st Century.* New York: Seven Stories, 2005.

Stewart S. Miller   *Wi-Fi Security.* New York: McGraw-Hill, 2003.

Daniel Minoli   *Hotspot Networks: Wi-Fi for Public Access Locations.* New York: McGraw-Hill, 2003.

Tom Negrino   *Mac OS X Unwired: A Guide for Home, Office, and the Road.* Sebastopol, CA: O'Reilly, 2003.

Jonathan E. Nuechterlein   *Digital Crossroads: American Telecommunications Policy in the Internet Age.* Cambridge, MA: MIT Press, 2005.

Ramjee Prasad   *From WPANs to Personal Networks: Technologies and Applications.* Boston: Artech House, 2006.

Ramjee Prasad, ed.   *Towards the Wireless Information Society.* Boston: Artech House, 2006.

Tapan K. Sarkar   *History of Wireless.* Hoboken, NJ: Wiley-Interscience, 2006.

Shahid K. Siddiqui   *Roaming in Wireless Networks.* New York: McGraw-Hill, 2006.

Clint Smith and John Meyer   *3G Wireless with WiMAX and Wi-Fi: 802.16 and 802.11.* New York: McGraw-Hill, 2005.

Teik-Kheong Tan — *The World Wide Wi-Fi: Technological Trends and Business Strategies.* Hoboken, NJ: Wiley-Interscience, 2003.

Peter Pericles Trifonas, ed. — *Communities of Difference.* New York: Palgrave Macmillan, 2005.

Periodicals

Jason Ankeny and Vince Vittore — "Cities Without Limits: How Wireless Is Galvanizing Small-Town America," *Wireless Review*, September 1, 2004.

Matthew Boyle — "The Really, Really Messy Wi-Fi Revolution: Silicon Valley Needs Wireless Internet to Boom. But Bringing It to the Masses Ain't Easy," *Fortune*, May 12, 2003.

Scott Bradner — "Unwiring Cities," *Network World*, September 13, 2004.

Andrew Brandt — "Your Wireless Network Needs a Security Update," *PC World*, March 2006.

Jennifer Brown — "Take the Office Poolside with Wi-Fi: Wireless Becomes Hot Ticket for Hotels as They Compete for the Attention of Business Travellers," *Computing Canada*, December 12, 2003.

Wally W. Conhaim — "A Revolution in Connectivity: Perspectives," *Information Today*, July/August 2003.

Phil Davies

"Companies Clamping Down on Wireless Workers Who Bypass Encryption; Freedom from Wires Carries a Heightened Risk of Hacking and Eavesdropping. Making Employees Take Wi-Fi Policies Seriously Requires Marketing—and a Threat of Consequences," *Workforce Management*, December 2003.

Sky Dayton and David Worrell

"Wireless Wealth: The Wi-Fi Revolution Is Coming. Find Out How Your Business Can Get In on the Ground Floor and Rope In Profits," *Entrepreneur*, July 2003.

Michael Gartenberg

"Wi-Fi: Why and Why Not," *Computerworld*, May 12, 2003.

Paul S. Henry and Hui Lou

"WiFi: What's Next?" *IEEE Communications Magazine*, December 2003.

W. Jackson

"New WiFi Spec Adds Stronger Encryption," *Government Computer News*, September 13, 2004.

Cassie Johnson

"Wireless Cities Bridge the Digital Divide," *Information Today*, April 2006.

Alicia Korney

"Cyber Crime Targets Firms of All Sizes, Panel Warns," *Providence Business News*, July 5, 2004.

Sharon M. Lightner and Lee Barken

"Lessons in Wi-Fi: Teachers and Students Learn About the Ups and Downs of In-Class Wi-Fi," *Mobile Business Advisor*, June 2003.

Paul Marks	"Cities Race to Reap the Rewards of Wireless Net for All; the Benefits Could Well Be Immense, but Turning a City into One Big Wi-Fi Hotspot Is Far from Straightforward," *New Scientist*, March 25, 2006.
Karen Lowry Miller	"The Wi-Fi Bubble," *Newsweek International*, August 4, 2003.
Michael J. Miller	"Wi-Fi Phones: A Natural Duo," *PC Magazine*, September 21, 2004.
Dan O'Shea	"More Heat for Hot Zones," *Wireless Review*, October 1, 2004.
Mike Outmesguine	"Be Your Own Hotspot: Turn a Backpack into a Portable, Solar-Powered Wi-Fi Hotspot, and Share a High-Speed Connection Anywhere," *Popular Science*, August 1, 2005.
Michael Schrage	"Crazy for Wi-Fi: Is It the New Revolution?" *Adweek Magazine's Technology Marketing*, May 2003.
Andy Serwer	"Wi-Fi Mania: When Whole Cities Are Public Hot Spots," *Fortune*, October 31, 2005.
Dan Tynan	"When Wi-Fi Won't Fly," *PC World*, October 2004.
Leo R. Versola	"Hot Spots Can Burn You," *Communications News*, October 2005.
Carol Wilson	"Wi-Fi Worries," *Telephony*, March 6, 2006.

Jia Lynn Yang   "It's Broadband. It's Wireless. It's
                       Cheap," *Fortune*, May 1, 2006.

Index